D1531807

IDENTITY THEFT

IDENTITY THEFT

PROTECTING YOURSELF FROM
AN UNPROTECTED WORLD

ETHAN POPE

MOODY PUBLISHERS
CHICAGO

© 2006 by
ETHAN POPE

All Scripture quotations, unless otherwise indicated, are taken from the *New American Standard Bible®*, Copyright ©1960, 1962, 1963, 1968, 1971, 1972, 1973, 1975, 1977, 1995 by The Lockman Foundation. Used by permission.

Scripture quotations marked NLT are taken from the *Holy Bible, New Living Translation,* copyright © 1996. Used by permission of Tyndale House Publishers, Inc., Wheaton Illinois 60189. All rights reserved.

Certified Financial Planner Board of Standards Inc. owns the certification mark CERTIFIED FINANCIAL PLANNER™, which it awards to individuals who successfully complete the CFP Board's initial and ongoing certification requirements.

This book is not intended to give SPECIFIC legal, tax, or investment counsel. Its purpose is to give general insights in the area of personal money management and identity theft prevention. Neither the author nor the publisher can take responsibility for the reader's decisions based on the information provided in this book. Due to changing technology and laws, it is recommended that you seek professional counsel for your individual circumstances.

Cover Design: DesignWorks Group Inc.
Cover Image: Tim Green
Editor: Jim Vincent

Library of Congress Cataloging-in-Publication Data

Pope, Ethan.
    Identity theft : protecting yourself from an unprotected world / Ethan Pope.
      p. cm.
    Includes bibliographical references.
    ISBN-13: 978-0-8024-0974-4
      1. Identity theft—United States. 2. Identity theft—United States—Prevention. I. Title.
    HV6679.P67 2006
    362.88--dc22

                                                            2006006117

We hope you enjoy this book from Moody Publishers. Our goal is to provide high-quality, thought-provoking books and products that connect truth to your real needs and challenges. For more information on other books and products written and produced from a biblical perspective, go to www.moodypublishers.com or write to:

Moody Publishers
820 N. LaSalle Boulevard
Chicago, IL 60610

ISBN: 0-8024-0974-1
ISBN-13: 978-0-8024-0974-4

1 3 5 7 9 10 8 6 4 2

Printed in the United States of America

It is a federal crime when someone:

"knowingly transfers or uses, without lawful authority, a means of identification of another person with the intent to commit, or to aid or abet, any unlawful activity that constitutes a violation of Federal law, or that constitutes a felony under any applicable State or local law."

The Identity Theft and Assumption Deterrence Act (1998)
18 U.S.C. 1028(a)(7)

QUICK FACTS

Identity theft is one of the fastest growing crimes in America and the top reported fraud of 2005.

80%: Americans who are concerned about identity theft.

10 million: Estimated number of Americans affected by ID thefts each year.

$50 billion: Dollars that FTC estimates are lost annually as a result of identity theft.

50 million: People at risk due to data being lost or stolen or misplaced by corporations.

175 hours and $800: The time and cost, on average, for each victim of ID theft to clear his or her name.

Sources: "Federal Trade Commission—Identity Theft Survey Report"; *USA Today,* www.usatoday.com/money/industries/technology/2005-03-02-datathieves-usat_x.htm; Money magazine, August 2005, 27; "Identity Theft Survival Guide," CNNMoney, www.money.cnn.com/2002/04/03/pf/q_identity/index.htm.

Contents

Acknowledgments

THANK YOU . . .

to everyone at **Moody Publishers** who continues to work on the Financial Alert Series. It's hard to believe this is already book number three in the series. It's an honor to be on the same team with you. My special thanks to Greg Thornton for your ongoing commitment to this series; to Janis Backing for publicity; to John Hinkley for marketing; and to Jim Vincent, my editor, for helping to make this book the best it could be; I know the readers will appreciate your polishing skills.

to **Judy** for being so vulnerable in explaining what it's like being a victim of identity theft. (Her story appears in chapter 2.) I learned more from listening to you than from the hundreds of articles I read on the topic.

to **Tim Starling** for meticulously reading the manuscript for computer, Internet, and technical accuracy. I appreciate your expertise in this area.

to **Brian Houston,** not only for reading the manuscript and providing me with great suggestions, but for your contagious enthusiasm for this project.

to **Janet:** *It's great to be identified as your husband.*

to **Natalie** and **Austin:** *I love being identified as "Dad."*

QUICK EVALUATION

High Risk Profile for Potential Identity Theft

Put a checkmark in the box before each statement listed below that is true for you.

❏ *I have family, friends, neighbors, or associates who are in some type of trouble.*
If you have any family members, friends, neighbors, or work associates who you know are always in financial trouble, unemployed, addicted to drugs, or have filed for bankruptcy recently—your level of risk has greatly increased. It has been documented that 50 percent of identity thefts (when the person can be identified) are committed by a family member, neighbor, friend, or work associate. If the person has access to your personal data, your level of risk for identity theft is higher than normal.

❏ *I have responded to an e-mail requesting personal data.*
If you have responded to an e-mail supposedly from your bank, investment company, credit card company, PayPal, or eBay providing a link for you to click on that takes you to a Web site requesting personal data such as your name, address, date of birth, and Social Security number—your level of risk has greatly increased. Now the thief has everything he/she needs to open credit card accounts, obtain loans, and eventually harm your good name.

❏ *My Social Security number is visible (checks, driver's license, ID cards).*
If you have your Social Security number printed on your checks, you have greatly increased the potential for identity theft. Now a thief has your name, address, phone number (if on the check), AND your Social Security number. In addition, if your driver's license number is the same as your Social Security number, your level of risk is even higher. Why? Just think of the number of times you have to provide your driver's license for identification.

❏ *I use online banking, online investing, or order products through the Internet.*
Presently it is too easy for a crook to access a financial account. The only thing between your account and a crook is a user name and password. Until we add better security, anyone (including myself) is at some level of risk. I am not saying online banking should not be used, yet it can open the door to abuse. If you do use online banking, you should monitor your accounts at least once every week—if not daily.

❏ *I do not shred all my mail.*
If you are not using a shredder daily to destroy all the mail you trash, including preapproved credit card applications, financial statements, and credit card statements, you are putting yourself at a higher level of risk for identity theft. Note the focus here is on *all* your mail and *daily*.

❏ *I use an unsecured mailbox (at home or work).*
If you place your outgoing mail in an unsecured mailbox at home or work, your potential for identity theft is higher than normal. In addition, if your incoming mail is placed in an unsecured mailbox at home or work, your risk is higher than normal.

❏ *Computer passwords: (1) I have not changed my passwords in the last three months, and/or (2) I use easy-to-remember passwords, and/or (3) I save passwords on my computer, and/or (4) I keep my password taped on my computer.*
Easy passwords are like your mother's maiden name, your middle name, your date of birth, your pet's name, or simply a series of numbers such as 12345. All any crook needs to log into your online account is your user name and password. That's all it takes to enter the private territory of a person's financial life. Also, saving passwords on your computer creates a higher risk. Friends, family, and coworkers can access your account easier if you save your password. Also, not changing your passwords puts you in a higher level of risk.

❏ *I have not installed antivirus and firewall software on my computer.*
In the world of computer viruses and invasive spyware, your computer must have protective software installed. If you don't use these protections and enter the world of the Internet or e-mail, your level of risk is elevated, compared to those who operate with antivirus and firewall software. Also check this box if you have the software installed on your computer but do not update it online daily (usually free with your subscription).

❏ *I do not store my financial records in a locked file cabinet.*
You are at risk if anyone has free access to your bank statements, investment statements, blank checks, and credit card bills. Everyone needs to use a locking filing cabinet. Locks on filing cabinets don't keep criminals out, but they will help keep your friends, neighbors, and work associates from snooping.

❑ ❑ *I do not order my free credit report three times per year.*

If you have never ordered your free credit report, how do you know what accounts or loans are in your name? You don't! There are three major credit reporting companies, and federal law requires each one to provide a free credit report annually. The best system is to request one free report from a different company every four months. In fact, if you have never ordered a free credit report, you earn double points for this one! I am serious—check two boxes for this one.

Bonus points:

❑ *I am a senior citizen.*

Someone age sixty-five or older is at a higher risk than the general population to become a victim of a scam. Many (but surely not all) senior citizens know very little about using a computer, identity theft, and common scams.

What's your score?

Although this high-risk profile is somewhat simplistic, it does provide a quick risk evaluation. Give yourself ten points (and for the question about ordering your free credit reports, twenty points) for each of the above that is true about you.

Write your score here: _____

What does your score represent?

If your score is 70, this means that you could be at a 70 percent or higher level of risk to become a victim of identity theft. And just because your score might be 0 percent does not mean you are at no risk. It means that the level of your risk is definitely very low—compared to most other people.

Circle your score and find your risk level for identity theft:

0%	10%	20%	30%	40%	50%	60%	70%	80%	90%	100%

Very Low   **Low**   **Moderate**   **High**   **Very Dangerous**

The Alert

HOW SAFE IS YOUR GOOD NAME?

J. EDGAR HOOVER, the notorious crime fighter who directed the FBI for forty-eight years, would be intrigued to learn about this new *invisible criminal wreaking financial havoc in America*: a criminal who never uses a gun, never enters a bank or home, yet has the ability to steal money right out of your bank account or go on a major spending spree using your good name and credit cards

Welcome to the twenty-first century . . . and *identity theft*. It's the fastest growing crime in America.

Maybe you've seen those identity theft commercials where a woman is talking like a man or a man is talking like a woman. Perhaps you've seen the one where a rough-looking man wearing a white T-shirt sitting in a chair is talking like a young girl who just went on a "fun" shopping spree. Or the one where the old lady with gray hair is talking like a younger man. You get this creepy feeling when you are watching those commercials.

Well, identity theft should give you a creepy feeling, because it's possible that some creep *this very moment* is using your good name to get a job, buy clothes, go on a cruise, or obtain a loan. It's also possible that the person was arrested last night and gave *your* name, *your* Social Security number, and *your* address to the police.

Initially, identity theft is like being robbed without even knowing it! You are feeling no pain—the doors on your home are still locked, your car is in your garage, all your credit cards are still in your wallet, and your checkbook is visible on your desk. No one stuck a gun in your face and asked you to hand over your wallet. In fact, it's possible you have been robbed every day for months and you still don't even know it—yet. *Oh, but you will.*

What begins as a painless crime will end with more pain and anxiety than you can ever imagine. Just talk to anyone who has had their identity stolen!

Yes, there is a new thief on the prowl. He's not after your jewelry, television set, or even your cash. What he's after is far more valuable—*your* good name, *your* Social Security number, *your* address, *your* mother's maiden name, *your* log-in name, *your* password, and *your* birth date.

These important pieces of personal data can provide the "keys" for an identity thief to open up credit card accounts in your name, buy cars and clothes, buy new TVs, go on cruises, work and avoid paying taxes, and even steal money right out of your bank or brokerage account.

To some criminals your Social Security number has become more valuable than gold. Who would have ever thought the day would come when crooks might dig through your nasty garbage just to obtain personal data—and have no interest in stealing your jewelry and television?

FINANCIAL ALERT, ALERT, ALERT

Is it really a big problem? Let me answer that question by offering the following revealing statistics.

- According to the Federal Trade Commission, the fastest growing crime in the United States was identity theft.[1]

- For the fifth year in a row [2000–2004], identity theft topped the list of complaints, accounting for 39 percent of the 635,173 consumer fraud complaints filed with the agency last year.[2]

- Credit card fraud was the most common form of reported identity theft, followed by phone or utilities fraud, bank fraud, and employment fraud.[3]

- Identity theft affects approximately 10 million Americans each year.[4]

My research has shown that *the majority of Americans are very concerned* about identity theft, yet *very few Americans know how to prevent it* or have taken serious steps to avoid identity theft.

How much of a wake-up call do *you* need before *YOU* begin to take action?

To talk to and read about those who have had their identity stolen, it appears to be just as painful as if they had been bitten by a poisonous snake. If I were to tell you there are poisonous snakes in your yard and in your workplace . . . what would you do? I trust you would find ways to eliminate the snakes and protect yourself!

If you doubt that identity theft bites as severely as does a venomous snake, just talk to someone whose identity has been stolen. *I did!* As I interviewed victims or read accounts in the newspaper of identify theft, I saw and heard:

- *Pain*—pain that is psychological, physical, emotional, and financial
- *Helplessness* during the process
- *Confusion* over what to do
- *Frustration* and *stress*
- *Concern* if this mess will ever be resolved
- *Anger* toward the thief and credit industry
- *Fear* of what might happen in the future
- *Outrage* at Congress for allowing lobbyists to keep legislation from being passed that would help solve the problem for most Americans

As you can see from the above, all you have to do is name the emotion and most victims of identity theft have experienced it. You put all of these feelings together and what you have is an explosive topic. I also learned that most victims of identity theft end up spending hundreds of hours and dollars trying to resolve the problem.

Those who have had their identity stolen feel violated. One victim even went so far as to say, "I was raped in some way." Another called the theft of his identity "the biggest hassle I've ever been part of in my life." The emotion and pain go deeper than anyone could ever imagine—and continue for months or years. Why? In some cases identity theft is an ongoing crime—compared to a single event such as your home being robbed or someone robbing you on the street. It's very hard for a victim to bring closure to identity theft.

THE SCOPE OF THE PROBLEM AND A RECOMMENDED SOLUTION

How big is the problem? *It's huge!* The Secret Service and FBI recently infiltrated a Web site that was buying and selling credit card numbers and identity documents online. In one case, twenty-eight people were arrested in seven countries. They were buying and selling two million stolen credit card numbers on a Web site. And four thousand people had purchased credit card numbers and other personal data on Web sites.[5] This is just one incident! The selling of numbers and personal data has become a big international business including ties to the Mafia.

The most surprising aspect of identity theft is that most identity theft problems could be avoided if Congress passed a simple law; yet our legislators are unwilling to act. We do applaud some states, however, that are creating state laws that offer good solutions. More on how we can solve the problem on the national level in chapter 8.

BUILDING A WALL OF PROTECTION

Identity Theft was written to help you build a wall of protection around your personal and financial data. Protecting yourself is really a simple concept: The harder you make it for a crook to obtain your personal data, the lower your risk of having your identity stolen.

It's not that difficult to build a wall of protection around your financial life. *You just need to know what to be doing and what not to be doing.* And there is no need to worry about the things you cannot control! This book is full of information, answers, and specific directives.

THE BIG QUESTIONS

I will be answering the four big questions that everyone is asking about identity theft.

- What is identity theft?
- How can I protect myself?
- What do I need to do if someone has stolen my identity?
- How can we solve the problem?

I worked hard to keep this a relatively simple book. You should be able to read it in one evening. *Sure hope that is true.*

Every person who has a bank account (it does not matter if it's online or not), investments, or a credit card is at some level of risk. Someone out there wants to steal your identity and have a good time at your expense.

All of us want to protect our good name. "A good name is to be more desired than great wealth" (Proverbs 22:1).

We are to be on the alert! Webster defines *alert* as: "watchful and ready, as in facing danger." This book is a specific call for all Americans to do just that—be on the alert!

With a little effort you can protect your good name in an unprotected world.

NOTES

1. www.money.cnn.com/2002/04/03/pf/q_identity/index.htm
2. www.ftc.gov/opa/2005/02/top102005.htm
3. Ibid.
4. CRS Report for Congress, Congressional Research Service, RS22082, "Identity Theft: The Internet Connection" (March 16, 2005).
5. www.usatoday.com/money/industries/technology/2005-03-02-datathieves-usat_x.htm

ONE

Top Ten Scams

WHAT SHOULD YOU BE ON THE ALERT FOR?

AS I READ ABOUT SOME of the most notorious scams while doing research for this book, I was somewhat surprised. All are deceitful, of course, but some are clever and really humorous. Well, not humorous to the person who is scammed, but humorous to some of us who read about their stories.

Yes, I can chuckle as I read about some of these scams, but be assured: I have great compassion and understanding *for anyone* who has been scammed—because over twenty years ago I was a victim!

MY STORY

The scam that I was caught in the middle of involved investing in silver futures, *which I knew absolutely nothing about at that time.* I received a phone call one evening at my home. The person on the other end of the phone was a great salesman and appeared to be very knowledgeable about his product. He asked me if I had ever invested in silver futures, and I answered, "No." During his sales presentation he gave me several examples of how a small amount of money could turn into big returns. He asked if I was interested in learning more; I said, "Yes."

Within a few days I received in the mail a slick brochure and another phone call. (I honestly cannot remember the exact dollar amounts, but to the best of my memory here is what happened during the next few weeks.) Initially, he convinced me to invest $1,000 just to see what might happen in the next few weeks. Well, I foolishly mailed a cashier's check to the address he provided. Within a week he called me back to let me know that my initial investment had doubled and was now worth $2,000. He strongly recommended that I consider investing $1,000 more.

There was always a sense of urgency—that if I didn't send the money immediately I might miss out on a great opportunity. (I did not know it twenty years ago, but "urgency" is one of the warning signs to detect a scam!) I bought into his hype and sent another $1,000. Within a few more weeks, my investment had already increased several thousand dollars. I ended up sending money for the third time. However, after my third check he discovered that I had reached my limit and had no plans to invest any more money with him. Then one day, he called to inform me that silver futures had greatly decreased and I had lost all but a few hundred dollars of my money.

I knew at that moment that I had been scammed. It was a sick feeling. I felt extremely embarrassed and like a fool. I knew better, but my desire to have a large return on my investment caused me to make decisions based on my emotions—not my mind.

The only person who has known about this during the past twenty years has been my wife, Janet. In fact, I find it really hard to believe that I am writing about it in this book. So, if you are ever talking to me, please don't bring it up (just kidding). I still find it very embarrassing. That's how most scam victims feel, embarrassed—*and scammers use this to their advantage because they know their victims seldom tell anyone, including the police!*

Hot Tip

ELIMINATE UNWANTED PHONE CALLS!
One of the best ways to eliminate the majority of telephone scams is to have an unlisted phone number. If they don't know your phone number, they will have a hard time calling you.

Based on my research for this book, you will find my list of the top ten scams—in no particular order. Be on the lookout for phone calls, e-mails, or letters coming your way. Half of winning the battle is knowing what to be on the alert for. Hopefully if any of the following scams come your way, alarms will be going off and red flags will be waving!

The intent of some of the scams listed below is to obtain your personal data in order to steal your identity. Others only have the intent of scamming you out of a few thousand dollars—not to steal your identity. Whether the goal is identity theft or stealing some of your money, all are wrong, and all are against the law.

SCAM #1
E-mail Verification of Personal Data

Just the other day I received the following "official-looking e-mail" from eBay.

FROM: **eBay**
TO: **Ethan Pope**
SUBJECT: eBay Inc: Update Your Account Records

Dear eBay Member,

We regret to inform you that your eBay account could be suspended if you don't re-update account information. To resolve this problem please visit the link below and re-enter your account information:

[I have removed the Web link.]

If your problem cannot be resolved your account will be suspended for a period of 24 hours; after this period your account will be terminated.

It looked and sounded authentic, *but it was a first-class scam.* It's one of the most common ways ID thieves try to get personal data. Here's another e-mail request I received today (as I was writing this chapter!):

FROM: Service@paypal.com
TO: Ethan Pope
SUBJECT: PayPal Account Suspension Notice

Dear Ethan,

We recently reviewed your account, and suspect that your PayPal account may have been accessed by an unauthorized third party. Protecting the security of your account and of the PayPal network is our primary concern. Therefore, as a prevention measure, we have temporarily limited access to sensitive PayPal account features.

Please click on the link below to confirm your information:

[I have removed the Web link.]

For more information about how to protect your account, please visit PayPal's Security Center, accessible via the "Security Center" link located at the bottom of each page of the PayPal website.

We apologize for any inconvenience this may cause, and appreciate your assistance in helping us maintain the integrity of the entire PayPal system. Thank you for your prompt attention to this matter.

Sincerely,
The PayPal Fraud Management Team

Several days earlier I received an unusual variation, supposedly from PayPal as well. The e-mail contained all the official logos, even the usual PayPal design and colors.

The e-mail read:

FROM: Service@paypal.com
TO: Ethan Pope
SUBJECT: Your payment has been sent to
sales@omegamove.com

This email is to confirm that you have paid $395.95 USD using PayPal.

This credit card transaction will appear on your bill as "PAYPAL OMEGAMOVE".

Shopping Cart Contents:
Item Name: Omega Men Watch – mint
Quantity: 1
Total: $395.85

If you haven't authorized this charge, click the link below to cancel the payment and get a full refund.

Dispute Transaction Link

Thank you for using PayPal.

What was my response to this supposedly alarming e-mail? I will have to admit, even though I am very familiar with financial scams, this one initially caught me off guard. My heart began beating faster for a few seconds before I realized this was just a different variation of an old scam to obtain my personal data. Then I simply hit the *delete* button! I knew exactly what this scammer was doing.

You will see scammers illegally using official logos of Visa, MasterCard, American Express, Discover, PayPal, eBay, and major banks, hoping you will respond. Don't let the official look and official warning scare you.

Never, never, never click on an e-mail link to verify personal data!

You will find more on this type of scam later in the book.

SCAM #2
Verification of Personal Data or Account

Any scammer can find your name, address, bank account number, bank name, and usually your phone number by looking at any check you have written. Let's see how a scammer who knows your name, address, phone number, and the name of your bank might use this information.

"Hello, Mrs. Nelson, this is Frank Moore with the First National Bank calling. I work in the fraud investigation department. How are you doing this afternoon?

"Now let me begin by saying there is no reason for you to be alarmed, but we have reason to believe that someone has been trying to electronically transfer funds out of your bank account. Because this appears to be an inside job, our phone call needs to remain confidential. Would you have just a few minutes to verify some information? Great.

"In order to verify that I am speaking with the right person, I need for you to give me your full name, date of birth, and your Social Security number." (Or, if they do not have your bank account number, they might ask you to look at your checkbook and read the numbers across the bottom of the check.)

Or, you might receive a call from someone stating they are calling from MasterCard or Visa with a question. The scammer has obtained your account number from a discarded statement or a photograph of your credit card (perhaps taken with a cell phone camera). All he needs now is the security number that is in your possession and protects from this kind of fraud. The deception is he is not asking for your credit card number: "Of course, I know your account number; now to verify I'm speaking to the account holder, please give me the three [or four] security digits printed on the back [or front] of your card."

This phone call can come from any of a variety of "institutions" attempting to verify information concerning your account. For example, you might receive a phone call from someone identifying himself as a representative of:

- your bank,
- Visa, MasterCard, or another credit card,
- an investment firm,
- the Social Security Administration,
- the human resources department at your workplace,
- the FBI, or
- the local police department.

However, *no institution* (financial, your workplace, or law enforcement) *will ever call you and ask you to provide personal data* on the phone. Therefore such a telephone inquiry should bring only one response. *Immediately hang up.* If you have strong reason to think it might be a legitimate inquiry, you can always call the financial institution or law enforcement agency. They will probably confirm that they did not and do not initiate such calls. Keep in mind that when *you* call your bank or financial institution, in the course of discussion they might ask for personal data; that is usually acceptable. What's the difference? *You initiated the call.*

Action Alert

GIVE NO PERSONAL DATA ON THE TELEPHONE

No financial institution or law enforcement agency will ever call you and ask you to provide personal data on the phone, nor will your workplace. Therefore, never give personal information over the telephone to any institution. Only give such information if you are in their office or when you call them directly at a legitimate number you have (from a business card, telephone book, or actual financial statement).

SCAM #3
Free Credit Report E-mails

Look out if you receive an e-mail offering a free credit report. When you click on the link, they will ask you to fill out a form with your name, address, birth date, name of spouse, place of employment, and Social Security number. They might even have a blank for you to fill in your mother's maiden name for security purposes.

Don't click on the link and fill out the form! If you do, you have just provided a crook with everything needed to steal your good name.

The form you filled out will go into a database with the names of thousands of others who filled out the form—only to be sold to identity theft criminals for some big bucks!

I will have more on requesting a free annual credit report later, but the bottom line is this: There is *only one place* you should request your free credit report, and that is www.annualcreditreport.com.

SCAM #4
Do Not Call List

The news media have given extended coverage about the "Do Not Call List," so practically everyone knows about this way to avoid unwanted phone calls from tele-marketers. Yet scammers have figured out a creative way to take advantage of this new program. They call you on the phone saying they are with the Federal Trade Commission (FTC) and ask if you would like to sign up for the FTC's "Do Not Call List." In order to sign up, you need to provide your Social Security number and address and verify your phone number, they explain.

However, the FTC does not call anyone asking if they want to sign up for the "Do Not Call List," nor is there a fee to sign up. You have to make the call or register online.

The two official ways to add your telephone number to the national "do not call" registry are: (1) Call the national registry at 1-888-383-1222 (be sure to call from the number you want to register); (2) go online at the official Web site, which is www.donotcall.gov.

Next are a couple scams in which the thief doesn't want your identification; he wants your money—now—and has clever ways to *have you send it* to him.

SCAM #5
The Infamous Nigerian E-mail Letter

If you have been using e-mail the last few years, it's about 99.9 percent likely that you have received the infamous Nigerian e-mail letter (or a similar solicitation from a government representative of another country). It comes in different types of appeals for help from a government, but here's the bottom line: It's an e-mail from a supposed official (or relative of an official) pleading for you to help them transfer large sums of money out of their country.

According to the FTC, this e-mail scam has reached epidemic proportions. The e-mail promises that you will receive up to 30 percent (or some other amount) of $10 million (or some other amount) if you will assist in a financial transaction using your bank account. Practically every e-mail or letter has a sense of urgency. The victim is asked to provide bank account numbers, blank letterhead, and invoices to help complete the transaction.

You might be thinking, *What idiot would respond to an e-mail like this?* Well, according to the Secret Service Web site, Americans have actually traveled to Nigeria to help complete the transaction. Some have been murdered or beaten. Those who make it home realize they have been scammed. The Secret Service indicates the scam "grosses hundreds of millions of dollars a year."[1]

SCAM #6
"You Have Won a Prize"

The phone call (or letter in the mail) goes something like this: "Congratulations, you have just won a cash prize of $100,000! No, I am not kidding, and this is not a prank phone call. . . . Now it is very important in order for you to receive your prize money that you follow my specific instructions or your prize money could be forfeited. In order for us to award and deliver your prize within 48 hours, you must send $1,000 (or another amount) in order to (1) complete the certification process, and (2) to cover the cost for one of our employees to personally deliver the check to your home. Tell me, how will it feel to hold a check for one hundred thousand dollars in your hand? Do you have a pen and piece of paper? Here is where you need to overnight the money . . . "

The person being scammed goes to the bank, obtains a casher's check, overnights the money, and goes home excited. After several days of no phone calls and no prize money being delivered, they realize they have been scammed.

Or if the scammer is not trying to have you send money but steal your identity, he might ask you to "simply" provide your Social Security number, date of birth, and mailing address.

Good people all over America fall for this scam or a similar prize scam every day. However, we seldom hear about it, because they are too embarrassed to tell family members, friends, or the police. And once again, the scammer counts on this fact.

Especially be on the lookout for letters or phone

calls about Canadian or Netherlands prize or lottery money. They are scams!

Just the other day I had lunch with a banker who told me about a woman in our city who was scammed out of $3,900. She did not received a phone call, but a letter in the mail stating that she was a winner in the Canadian lottery. She could not remember signing up for the Canadian lottery, and just assumed she had filled out a form somewhere and dropped it in a box. They tricked her into sending $3,900 in order to collect her prize money—money that did not exist and would never come.

SCAM #7
Failure to Report for Jury Duty

Here is another scam intent on stealing your identity. Posing as a clerk for a local court, the scammer calls to inform you that you failed to appear for jury duty yesterday and that a warrant has been issued for your arrest.

You immediately begin to explain that you never received a jury duty notice in the mail and there must be a misunderstanding. The clerk explains in a very firm and convincing voice that you are in big trouble and that the judge is tired of dealing with "no show jurors." Now that you are caught off guard (and flustered), the scammer, in what appears to be a moment of compassion, says this can possibly be cleared up on the phone if you can verify the following information: your Social Security number, home address, occupation, and date of birth. Wanting to avoid an arrest and fine (and without thinking), you provide the requested data to the caller.

The scammer now has what he wants and informs you there must have been a mistake. The court clerk apologizes and informs you that the warrant for your arrest will be withdrawn. You hang up the phone and take a big sigh of relief— *never imagining you have just been scammed.*

Jury duty scams have been reported in Oregon, Washington State, Michigan, Texas, Ohio, Arizona, Illinois, Pennsylvania, and Minnesota. I am sure more states are being added to the list on a regular basis.

SCAM #8
Surveys

Be very cautious of phone surveys and on-the-street surveys. I once read about a consumer advocate group that made a disturbing finding in one experiment. Wanting to find out just how much information people would be willing to provide for the chance of winning a couple of tickets, they went out on the streets offering a chance to win "free tickets" to a very popular play. They were very shocked at how most people on the street were so willing to provide personal data.

Never give certain personal data when responding to any survey, whether on the phone or in person. Specifically, do not provide any of the following:

- Social Security number

- credit card numbers

- name of bank

- bank account number

- number of credit cards you possess

- name of your favorite credit card (This answer will tell them a specific credit card you use and that you use it regularly.)

- home address

- place of employment

Surveyors have no valid reason to be asking for any of your personal data. I see no problem with answering questions about your favorite football team, your favorite color, the number of books you read last year, or the last time you ordered vanilla ice cream. Who cares? No big deal.

The trickery scammers use in surveys is to ask indirect questions to obtain the data they want. For example, they might ask, "What is your favorite credit card company?" This is an indirect question that will tell them what credit card you like to use. You might be more cautious if they asked, "What credit cards do you use?" or "Will you show me what credit cards you have in your wallet?"

SCAM #9
Overseas Job Offer

The final two scams again seek to have you send money directly to the crook (no identity theft needed!). I recently interviewed a woman whose husband was scammed by responding to an overseas job offer. Here is her story.

"My husband went on the Internet because he was trying to find an offshore job. He eventually found a company that was offering a high-paying job with an American oil company located in Nigeria. After a few e-mails, he received a contract in the mail confirming his salary, details of when he would leave the States, when he would return home, and when he would receive his visa and passport materials in the mail.

"Of course, it looked like a very official contract offer. We looked at it, talked about it, and actually said, 'This is too good to be true.' The first thing we had to do was to send two cashier's checks for $25 each to Nigeria. Next, the person "representing the company" told us that we needed to send $2,250 using Western Union in order for him to process my husband's worker's permit. This would allow my husband to be able to leave the United States and work in Nigeria.

"We were also told that when my husband began working, the monthly salary was to be electronically deposited into our bank account, so we had to fax him our bank account and routing number."

The couple faxed the information and later did receive a check in the mail for $12,000. They were told that was an advance on the husband's first-month salary. Then they were instructed to deposit the $12,000 check and to return $9,000 to finalize all of the necessary paperwork. But the wife hesitated, because she noticed something peculiar.

"When I examined the $12,000 check, it appeared to be phony. We later found out it was. I am glad to say that we did not send the $9,000 as instructed. But, we did lose the $2,250 plus the initial $50 plus all the overseas shipping charges."

A variation of this overseas-job scam has you hired by an overseas company that will let you work for them while living in the United States. A Web site or e-mail arrives announcing you can "Earn Big Bucks Working At Home." A foreign company needs a work-at-home assistant to help with financial transfers from America to their company overseas, the copy reads. It takes too long to clear American checks overseas. The company would like to send you a batch of checks each week from customers in America in the amount of $2,000 to $100,000.

All you have to do is deposit the checks into your account and wire 95 percent of the funds to a foreign bank. Your commission is 5 percent. I can only assume that in order to test your "trustworthiness" they might send you a check for only $1,000 the first week. After you receive the check, you make the deposit and transfer by wire (not personal check) $950, and you get to keep $50. You are thinking this is too easy and calculating that your commission will be $5,000 when you "process" checks totaling $100,000.

But, guess what. The first check you receive and process for $1,000 is bogus and bounces in a few days. Bottom line: you just transferred *$950 of your money* to an overseas bank account. After you finally realize what happened, you get this sick feeling in your stomach.

SCAM #10
IRS "E-Audit"

Anytime you see something from the Internal Revenue Service, it gets your attention. What if you received an e-mail with the subject line reading: "IRS E-Audit"? That subject line would receive anyone's attention.

The body of the e-mail explains that, in order to avoid an assessment of interest and penalties, you need to provide the requested information within forty-eight hours. The scam uses the term "e-audit" to make you think the IRS is doing audits online.

They might ask you to send information such as your Social Security number, last year's W-2 earnings amount, and other personal data. It's a scam! The e-mail will even include the IRS logo to make it look more official. Be assured, *the IRS will never* send you an e-mail asking for you to respond by providing personal data such as your Social Security number and other confidential information.

RULES OF CONDUCT

Well, there you have it, some of the most common scams today. There are many others that I did not list that you need to be on the lookout for. Following is a list of my "Scam-Buster Rules of Conduct." Follow these rules of conduct and you will be able to avoid most scams and identity theft.

SCAM-BUSTER RULES OF CONDUCT

RULE 1

Be on the alert when talking to strangers on the phone, in person, or through e-mail.

RULE 2

Never provide personal data (name, address, Social Security number, credit card numbers, debit card numbers, financial account numbers, etc.) to *anyone calling* you on the telephone.

RULE 3

Never provide personal data to anyone showing up at your door, no matter how official they might look or how many identification badges they have hanging on their pocket.

RULE 4

Never provide personal data in e-mail or links provided in e-mails.

RULE 5

Never send money to anyone calling you saying you have won a prize, or anyone asking for money for handling charges—unless you have initiated the call.

RULE 6

It's acceptable (and advised) to hang up on a caller who refuses to take "no" for an answer.

RULE 7

Remember, the person may not be who he says he is; just because someone identifies himself as working for your bank, credit card company, or the government, does not guarantee he is.

RULE 8

Do not be intimidated by a threatening caller or e-mail warning that your account will be closed if you do not respond with requested information.

RULE 9

Remember, *if it looks too good to be true, it probably is.*

RULE 10

If you have been scammed, don't be embarrassed to tell a friend, family member, and the police.

PROTECTING SENIORS

Senior citizens have become the focus of many thieves who are looking to scam them out of their money or steal their identity. Why would they focus on senior citizens? There are several key reasons. Here are a few of them:

1. *Loneliness.* A lot of senior citizens (especially shut-ins) are very lonely people. People seldom come and visit them, and few call just to talk. So when a kind voice on the other end of the phone begins to express interest in them and is even willing to talk to them for an hour, the senior citizens begin to develop a trust in the person calling. It is not uncommon for a scammer to call once a day or once a week, for weeks, developing the relationship before the scam takes place. As he develops the trust, the scammer often tricks the senior citizen into providing additional family information (such as the death of a spouse and who handles their financial matters). The higher the level of trust, the bigger the scam!

2. *The promise of money.* Many senior citizens are living on a fixed income and are easily tempted by the potential to receive a large cash prize or additional income. Social Security is the only source of income for approximately 22 percent of the elderly, and 66 percent of senior citizens receive half their total income from Social Security.[2] In 2005 the average Social Security beneficiary check was only $955 per month.

3. *Kindhearted.* Many senior citizens are taken advantage of because of their kind hearts. They know what it is like to have pain and heartache, and the scammer knows what strings to pull—just to get them to send money. The scammer might be "representing a charity" and using emotions to obtain a response.

4. *Politeness.* Most senior citizens were not raised to be rude—by hanging up the phone before the other person has said good-bye. I know it used to disturb my mother when she had to hang up on a caller. I did my best to convince her that many of those calling her were crooks and taking advantage of people.

5. *Fear.* Most scammers are very polite and don't threaten or intimidate their victims, but some do. How would you feel if you were a senior citizen living alone and you received a threatening phone call?

6. *Mental ability.* Some of the most intelligent and sharpest people I know are senior citizens, but many are not as mentally sharp as they used to be. Brilliant business men and women who years ago could think quickly and clearly now take longer to analyze the situation and make sound decisions. Crooks are eager to take advantage of this weakness.

7. *Record keeping.* Some senior citizens used to reconcile their bank statement every month and did so for forty years. However, due to poor eyesight or a lack of interest, they stopped doing it. A lack of proper record keeping opens the door to fraudulent activities going unnoticed for months or years.

ACTION ALERT

INFORM SENIOR CITIZENS YOU KNOW

Be sure you sit down and talk with senior citizens you know about common scams and help them to understand what is at risk. A good list to review would be the top ten scams and the "Scam-Buster Rules of Conduct" in this chapter. Maybe you can offer to teach a "Scam Buster" seminar for senior citizens in your church or community.

Let's help to protect the senior citizens that we know and love.

Whether the victim is a senior citizen or a college graduate just into his first job, these scams are dangerous because they can bring financial disaster and long-lasting upheaval to people's lives. How much upheaval? The next chapter lets us see the shocking consequences of identity theft in the lives of Americans today and why it's important to take wise steps to prevent ID theft in your own life.

NOTES

1. www.secretservice.gov/alert419.shtml
2. Ethan Pope, *Social Security?* (Chicago: Moody, 2005), 24.

T W O

The Shock

WHAT REALLY HAPPENS
WHEN YOUR IDENTITY IS STOLEN?

IN NEIGHBORHOODS ALL ACROSS America, real people just like you and me are becoming victims of identity theft—*by the millions.* Most victims love their families, work hard, and never harm anyone—but now they are experiencing the pain of what it means to have their identity stolen or to be a victim of financial fraud.

Here are two of their stories . . .

BEFORE HIS VERY EYES

George's astonishing story was reported recently on the front page of *USA Today.* Here's how the article began:

> When he logged on to his Ameritrade account earlier this year, George Rodriguez caught a cybercrook in the act of cleaning out his retirement nest egg.
>
> He watched, horrified, as the intruder in quick succession dumped $60,000 worth of shares in

Disney, American Express, Starbucks and 11 other blue-chip stocks, then directed a deposit into the online account of a stranger in Austin.

"My entire portfolio was being sold outright before my eyes," recalls Rodriguez, 41, a commercial real estate broker who alerted Ameritrade in time to stop the trades.

Rodriguez had just experienced a tech-savvy consumer's worst nightmare. But it's the reality of the digital world we live in: Everyone is now at risk of becoming the victim of an Internet-based crime."[1]

What if this had been your story? The alarming part is your story could be appearing on the front page of *USA Today* next week unless you learn how to build a wall of protection around your personal data and financial assets. However, be encouraged: In the coming chapters you will learn how to build your wall of protection.

JUDY'S STORY

Judy's story never made the front page of *USA Today*, but she is a recent victim of identity theft. I learned more about the emotional side of identity theft by talking with Judy in one hour than I learned from reading hundreds of articles about the topic.

The Phone Call

"One morning I received a call from a collection agency saying that I had not paid my cell phone bill and that I owed them some two or three thousand dollars! I said,

'My cell phone bill?' *At that time I didn't even have a cell phone.* So I said, 'Sorry, you must have the wrong person. This is a mistake.' Then he said, 'Now, now, Judy.' He was being very condescending. So I said, 'Well, what do you want, because I don't even own a cell phone?' I think that is what got his attention.

"After we had talked awhile on the phone, then he used the words *identity theft.* I could tell that he was disgusted because he wasn't going to get any money. In his eyes, this was bad news for him . . . not necessarily for me!

"At that same moment, when I realized I was a victim of identity theft, my anxiety level immediately shot up and I began thinking, 'Oh no, not me!'"

Judy's Emotions

"When I realized what this all meant, my heart literally sank. Then I began to think, 'What else is going on that I don't know about? This could be like the tip of an iceberg —what else is underneath? What else have they done?'

"It was an awful, awful realization that something bad was happening to me. It's really hard to express.

"I was scared to death! You hear about this happening to everybody else; this is not supposed to happen to me. You read about identity theft in newspapers and magazines and you are thinking, 'Well, I protect my Social Security number and I am very careful, so it won't happen to me.' *Wrong!*"

Her Case

"Here is what I found out concerning my case. A young girl and some of her friends went to a cell phone store in

Maryland (that's not where I live) and said that she needed to set up an account for her grandmother. When the sales clerk asked why her grandmother wasn't with her, she told the clerk her grandmother could not speak. Now when I heard this story, I am thinking, 'What fool would open a cell phone account for a grandmother who couldn't talk?' I was so disgusted I told the cell phone company, 'You guys need a brain.'

"What I have learned is that you get very little help from anyone—the police, credit bureaus, or companies. You feel like you are on your own—*and you are*. No one wants to help you! I did exactly what all those articles tell you to do, but it was still hard being on your own."

When Judy first went to her local police department to report the identity theft, they basically said, "So, what do you want us to do?" Surprised, Judy said, "What do you mean? You are supposed to help me with this!" The bottom line: The police would not file a report.

"I realized that I was on my own. I had to do all the research, make all the phone calls, do most of the investigations and all the legwork. I was very surprised and disappointed at this point.

"However, I did find the detective in the local police department in Maryland very helpful. He would talk with me on the phone, did some investigation work for me, and even went to check out the address where the cell phone bill was being sent to—a parking lot. The police in Maryland assume the young girl obtained my Social Security number, name, and address off my driver's license (in another state)."

One day Judy spent an entire morning on the phone talking to the collection agency, a credit bureau, and the cell phone company. "But nobody wanted to give me any information about the theft because they were afraid I was going to be like a crazy person. One person actually said to me, 'How do we know you are not going to come in here with a gun and begin shooting?' And I said, 'All I am trying to do is straighten out a situation with my identity being stolen.' The cell phone company was no help at all. They kept saying, 'We have turned this over to a collection agency. Talk to them.' I wanted to get to the bottom of this, and what I needed was information. It was ridiculous. They basically ignored me."

The Fraud Alert

"The best thing I did was to put a fraud alert on my credit report. If someone tries opening an account or making a purchase in your name, the store has to call you. As soon as I filed the fraud alert with the three credit bureaus, I had three phone calls from businesses. 'Are you trying to buy a computer?' I answered, 'No, but stop them and don't let them go anywhere!' They said in order to hold someone they would need something on official stationery from a police department.

"I said, 'What? You have got to be kidding me!' So I immediately got in my car and drove to the police station and said, 'I placed a fraud alert with the credit bureaus, and I just received a phone call informing me that someone in another state is trying to buy a computer in my name. You need to call this number and send the store something official on your letterhead so they will hold them.

"They looked at me like I was crazy. The officer said, 'Well, I am sorry, but this is out of our jurisdiction.

We don't do those things.' I said, 'There is a person sitting in this store using my name and Social Security number and trying to buy a computer, and you are not going to help me?' I was so mad! So I said, 'Give me your stationery, and I will fax it myself!' I was totally frustrated at this point! The person who was using my identity was sitting in a store, and no one would arrest her."

Judy's conclusion? "No one wants to help," whether the police, Social Security office, or the mobile phone company. "They would say, 'Well, this is not my job' or 'This is not in my jurisdiction,' or 'Sorry, my hands are tied.' People just did not seem to care and that was very disappointing to me.

"As far as I know, they have never caught the crook. They had an opportunity, but missed it!"

SOME ADVICE

Judy's advice to any victim of identity fraud is, "Realize you have to do all the work yourself. No one is going to do it for you. And, just don't take no for an answer! I was very diligent to get the information I needed because I realized at that point the police were not going to help me, and I needed to find out who would help me. You might have to call the same place four or five times and talk to different people in order to get all the information you need. Be persistent!"

Judy has adopted four strategies to avoid having her identity being stolen again. Most important, she says, is that she requests her free credit reports three times a year "to see if there is anything on it that should not be on it." She also shreds all her mail, has replaced her Social Security number on her driver's license with a state ID number, and makes few purchases on the Internet.

Looking back once more at her feelings, Judy says, "I had read articles and knew identity theft happened to people, but I had never lost my purse, and I thought it was one of those things that would not happen to me. That's why I initially was in denial when it happened to me.

"During my experience I felt a wide range of emotions . . . frustrated, dissatisfied, and angry. But, the best word would be *abandoned*. . . . You are trying to prove, 'that's not me' and do all the right things to solve the problem, but nobody would help you. . . . *You feel abandoned by the very people who should be protecting you and helping you.*

IT CAN HAPPEN TO ANYONE

The stories of George and Judy are only two examples out of millions of financial fraud and identity theft cases. What did we learn? Identity theft is painful and scary and can happen to practically anyone.

But, exactly what is identity theft or financial fraud, and how does it occur? We will explore the answer to those questions in the next five chapters.

NOTE

1. Bryon Acohido and Jon Swartz, "Cyber Safecrackers Break into Online Accounts with Ease," *USA Today,* November 3, 2005, 1A.

THREE

The Theft

HOW CAN SOMEONE STEAL YOUR IDENTITY?

IDENTITY THEFT CAN BE DEFINED in a variety of ways, but the best way to explain it is by giving several examples of outcomes of having your identity stolen. Your good name (identity) can be illegally used by another person to do the following:

- *Obtain credit card(s) in your name.* In this common form of identity theft, someone obtains a credit card in your name, makes purchases, and leaves you with the past-due bills. All a person needs to accomplish this task is a little information about you and a new credit card will be issued in your name and under your Social Security number.

- *Activate a cell phone.* As we learned from Judy's story, someone can activate a cell phone in your name, use it for a few months, and leave you with the bill. This one should go under the heading "dumbest criminals," because all phone numbers dialed are stored in a computer database and can be traced. All the police have to do (if they are willing) is locate the people the crook frequently talked to, cross-check a few phone numbers, and catch the offender.

- **Sign a lease.** People with bad credit have a hard time leasing a home or apartment—and for good reason. They have a history of not paying their rent. So the identity thief gives the potential land-lord your name and Social Security number, which generates a great report. He then can stay in the home or apartment for three or four months before being evicted. He or she is evicted not because you or the police have caught up with the crook, but because the impostor didn't pay the rent. Some may indeed have good intentions to pay the rent, but using your good name does not transform their poor money management habits.

- **Obtain medical care.** If a thief obtains a fake ID, the name of your health insurance provider and your Social Security number, it is possible he or she could obtain medical care under your good name and leave you with the bill.

- **Purchase a car.** How would you like to find out someone purchased a car using your good name? It's possible some thief will actually go so far as to obtain a car loan using your identity.

- **Open bank accounts.** With your name and Social Security number, an ID thief can open a bank account with a $100 deposit. Once the new checks arrive, they go out and write bad checks all over town until they (actually you) get placed on a bad check list. Thanks to the Patriot Act, banks are now required to verify your identity by checking driver's licenses or other forms of identity with a picture. This does help, but it does not solve the problem, because people can create fake IDs.

- **Secure a job.** Other impostors have been known to secure a job under your name. You might be wondering, "Why would they do that?" The answer: to avoid paying taxes for the income they earned, or perhaps to allow an illegal alien to find work. You will only find out about this one when the IRS sends you letters stating that your reported income did not match your income reported by your employers.

- **Create a driver's license.** Since your driver's license is used frequently for identification purposes, thieves find ways to create and use fake ones.

This list is not all-inclusive, but it gives you a good idea of how someone can steal and use your identity.

As if these abuses aren't enough, your identity can be used as an alias when someone commits a crime. A thief may be put in jail—but booked under your name! *Kiplinger's* magazine reported an incident in which police showed up at a person's house, handcuffed, and arrested him because he did not show up for a scheduled court date. He spent two nights in jail before the police determined they had the wrong guy.[1] *Now, that's scary.*

DEFINING IDENTITY THEFT

We have defined identity theft through its outcomes, but we can also define the phrase by its three components.

Identity theft takes place when (1) another person (2) pretends to be you and (3) commits an unlawful act. In certain situations it can even become a federal crime. According to the Identity Theft and Assumption Deterrence Act of 1998, it is a federal crime when someone "knowingly transfers or uses, without lawful authority, a means of identification of another person with the intent to commit, or to aid or abet, any unlawful activity that constitutes a violation of Federal law, or that constitutes a felony under any applicable State or local law."

LEARNING YOUR IDENTITY HAS BEEN STOLEN

How do most victims find out their identity has been stolen? If someone has stolen your identity and abused your good name, here is how you might find out about it:

- You are denied a home mortgage.

- You are denied a new credit card.

- You are denied a car loan.

- You are denied school loans.

- You are denied a line of credit.

- You are denied medical care.

- You are denied when trying to pay with a personal check.

- You are arrested for a crime you did not commit.

- You are rejected for a job you have applied for.

- You are the recipient of collection agency phone calls.

- You are the recipient of collection letters.

- You find out by checking your credit report (more about this one later).

When a person is rejected for a loan or something else, she might be thinking, "There must be a mistake. You are talking to the wrong person." Mistakes can and do happen. But being denied something financially is probably the sign of financial fraud, if you know you have good credit.

HOT TIP

CREDIT CARD FRAUD VERSUS IDENTITY THEFT

There is actually a debate over exactly what is identity theft. Many articles and stories are confusing financial fraud with identity theft. What's the difference?

Credit card fraud occurs when a person obtains your credit card number and uses it to make a fraudulent purchase. Just because someone steals your credit card number and makes a fraudulent purchase *does not mean* that your identity has been stolen.

Identity theft is when a person obtains either your name, date of birth, address, or Social Security number and uses that data to do one or more of the following: open up credit card account(s) or bank account(s), obtain a fraudulent loan(s), secure a job, or lease rental property. Identity theft is not limited just to the list provided above.

However, in the Identity Theft and Assumption Deterrence Act of 1998, Congress instructed the Federal Trade Commission to label credit card fraud as identity theft.

No matter what you want to call it, identity theft or financial fraud is something you hope and pray never happens to you, anyone in your family, or anyone you know.

On the following pages we will focus on how you can begin building a wall of protection around your financial life.

NOTE

1. Kristin Davis, "But, Officer, That Isn't Me," *Kiplinger's,* October 2005, 87.

Prevention

WHAT CAN YOU BE DOING
TO PROTECT YOUR GOOD NAME?

IMPLEMENT A PLAN, and you can prevent most identity theft and financial fraud. Developing a plan is worth it. Remember, just one careless mistake could end up costing you hundreds of hours of work to reclaim your good name.

Let me encourage you to view your efforts to protect your good name like *building a wall of protection—and everything preventive you do is like adding a brick. The more you do, the bigger your wall of protection becomes.* The "Wall of Protection" chart (next page) shows twenty ways to protect your name in our unprotected world. These twenty preventives will help you reach your goal—to minimize your level of risk for identity theft.

On the following pages you will find information about how to build your wall of protection. I will be discussing things you should and should not be doing. In this chapter we will look at four foundational bricks that build security at (1) home, (2) work, (3) on your computer, and

Your Wall of Protection

ID Insurance	Avoiding Scams	Action Alerts	Being on Alert
Your Statements	Credit Cards	Unsolicited Mail	Credit Reports
While Traveling	On Telephone	Your Investments	In Public Places
Writing Checks	ID Cards	Applications	U.S. Mail
At Home	At Work	Your Computer	On the Internet

(4) on the Internet. Let's begin by taking a look at things you do at home and at work.

PROTECTING YOURSELF AT HOME

Use Your Shredder—Daily

Remember the saying, "An apple a day keeps the doctor away"? Using your shredder every day will help keep an identity thief away.

Note, I said *help*, not guarantee. As we will learn later in the book, your good name can be stolen in a variety of ways—one being right out of your trash can. Remember my interview with Judy, a victim of identity theft? She said, "And of course I shred anything and everything that comes through the door (laugh)."

As I mentioned in *Cashing It In*, the first book in this Financial Alert series, a commercial-grade shredder is a more important item to own in your home than a refrigerator. Shred each piece of mail and every financial statement you plan to trash that contains any personal information on it (name, address, phone numbers, account numbers, and/ or Social Security number). In fact, there is no reason why any mail coming to your house or office should end up in your garbage can without being shredded first.

Be sure you purchase a good crosscut paper shredder. Don't go with an inexpensive $19.95 model that shreds only two pieces of paper at a time. Not only will you end up seldom using it, but the motor will burn up in a few weeks because you were trying to shred more than two sheets of paper at a time. Expect to spend $100 or more on a really good shredder—one that will shred ten-plus sheets of paper or entire unopened envelopes! You know the envelopes I am talking about, those "You Are Preapproved" credit card mailings.

I saw an ad on TV this week for a shredder that even shreds CD disks. *Now that's a real man's shredder!* Be sure it's no problem to shred papers with staples. An automatic "on/off" feature is also nice. Like I said earlier, the best shredders crosscut or make confetti out of your paper, not just cut them into strips. Yes, the bigger and tougher the monster shredder, the better—*the more you will use it!* Hey, you can even make the daily shredding of your mail an exciting family event.

Never Recycle

Never throw any of your mail or financial statements in a paper recycle bin at home (or at work). Shred it and discard it with your regular trash.

Terms You Should Know

DUMPSTER DIVING

Identity thieves will actually take the time to go through your stinking garbage looking for credit card applications, bank statements, old credit card bills, old credit cards, and investment statements. Some will drive down the street or alley and throw your bag of garbage into their car and go home to sort through it.

It really doesn't matter to the thief if your statement has five-day-old spaghetti smeared all over it, as long as the credit card name, address, and numbers are readable. *Now that's gross.*

In offices, some don't even have to sort through all the nasty garbage. They might see a discarded credit card bill a fellow employee simply tossed into the trash can.

The old saying has never been truer: "One man's trash is another man's treasure."

Purchase and Use a Locking File Cabinet

In addition to having a shredder in your home, you should consider purchasing a filing cabinet that locks. A filing cabinet lock will never keep a determined thief out, but it will keep a potentially dishonest (or even honest) person from viewing your personal data. I've read a number of articles that stated that family members, neighbors, in-home employees, or workers have been known to steal personal data—employees like house-keepers, babysitters, or pet walkers. All it takes is a few seconds for someone to write down credit card numbers or Social Security numbers.

What do you need to keep locked up? Let me give you a few examples:

- automobile title
- new bank checks
- bank statements
- birth certificates
- bills and invoices
- credit card statements
- financial statements
- insurance policies
- Social Security card
- any personal data

HOT TIP

WHO TO LOOK OUT FOR

When the perpetrator could be identified:

- 32 percent were family members;
- 24 percent were strangers outside the workplace;
- 18 percent were friends, neighbors, in-home employees;
- 13 percent were company employees with access to personal data;
- 4 percent were coworkers; and
- 8 percent were someone else.

SOURCE: CRS Report for Congress, RS22082, March 16, 2005

PROTECTING YOURSELF AT WORK

Be Alert at Work

Remember to keep your guard up at work! As mentioned in "Terms You Should Know," dumpster diving takes place not only at your home but also in your office building. In reality, dumpster diving is easier to do in an office building or behind the building in a dumpster than at your home.

At work, have you ever opened a bill, credit card solicitation, or financial statement and, once you paid it or finished reading it, simply threw it in the trash? It's okay to open personal mail at work before/after work hours, during a break, or during lunch. But it's not okay to trash your personal mail without shredding it first! Use the same approach as you would protecting your mail at home. Remember, over 50 percent of known identity thieves are a work associate, neighbor, or family member. *Now that's shocking!*

Also remember not to use an unsecured mail drop box at work. A secure mailbox is not an open box where employees deposit personal mail. That may be okay for business mailings, but your personal mail needs more protection. Your personal mail is secure at your workplace only if there is a slot with a secure lid (or mail receptacle) and one person who is assigned to transport it to the local postal office. (For more information on having a secure mailbox at home and work, read "Install a Secure Mailbox" in chapter 5.

Practice Office Safety with Personal Belongings

Always keep personal belongings out of sight. Whether it is a wallet, purse, or even a prepaid calling card (to avoid charging your work for long-distance personal calls), use your desk drawers to avoid passersby and even coworkers from being tempted to look, or even snatch. If your drawer has a key, use it to secure items when you leave the work area. If storing in a filing cabinet, be sure to keep that cabinet locked.

Women need to be especially careful with purses,

which often contain much more than just a wallet. (A checkbook and perhaps a bill or financial statement may be inside.) Store your purse in a safe place. Don't provide anyone with an easy opportunity to steal it or plunder through it looking for personal data.

I know of one bank where if the branch manager finds a purse out in the open he might take it to his office. Then at the end of the workday, one of his employees will come to his office and say, "Brian, where's my purse?"

Practice Office Safety with Your Computer

Here are some reminders for using an office computer. (The next section will recommend safeguards for using your computer at home.) If you use the workplace computer for personal business during breaks, don't tape any personal passwords on your computer, and be sure to log off of any Web site you visit. Also be sure to load antivirus and firewall protection software on your workplace computer. Viruses, which are spread by bogus e-mail links and downloads, can damage your computer hardware and software programs, and even redirect personal information to an outside watcher. And without firewalls, an intruder can spy on your information and even intercept personal data. (There's more on antivirus and firewall protection in the next section.)

You might be thinking, "If I am part of a larger computer network, am I safer online or not?" Well, it all depends. If your company operates on a network, there is a good chance they are doing everything possible to protect you and your company by using antivirus software and firewall software. However, no software can keep you from clicking on a bogus Web link at the bottom of an e-mail.

PROTECTING YOUR HOME COMPUTER

Install Antivirus Software

In the world of computer viruses—which are typically transported to your machine by e-mail (and sometimes downloads from bogus Internet Web sites)—every computer needs to be protected with antivirus software. The cost is relatively inexpensive, and the upgrades are simple to do. You can even schedule your computer to automatically do upgrades online. Since new viruses are discovered practically every day, why not take full advantage of the service you are paying for and upgrade daily? It costs the same if you upgrade daily or monthly!

Install Firewall Software

Firewall software helps keep your computer secure from an evil intruder. It attempts to do exactly what it says: Build a security wall around your computer data, so you won't get burned by an outsider raiding your computer and taking important data or implanting a destructive virus into your computer.

Firewall software becomes even more critical if your computer is always connected to the Internet. Without a firewall, a hacker could invade your computer, access private data, and even destroy all the files on your computer once he gets what he is looking for.

If you use a dial-up Internet connection to check your e-mail and browse a few Web sites for about fifteen minutes each day, your level of risk is lower. However, if you are connected to the Internet twenty-four hours a day, seven days a week (24/7), the potential for a hacker to break into your computer and steal personal data greatly increases!

If you really want to decrease your level of risk, do not keep your computer online 24/7. Disconnect from the Internet when you are not using it or especially when you finish for the day. If you want to remain connected to the Internet 24/7, consider storing your financial data on a second computer.

Use Two Computers

Let me emphasize that final point of using a second computer to keep your financial data away from intruders. I realize this recommendation may be cost prohibitive for most families. Still, consider using two computers, making the second one an economical, bare-bones model. After all, you're dedicating the computer to do just one main task. Only go online briefly to check accounts or do financial transactions with this second computer. Do not use your "financial computer" for regular Internet surfing or e-mails. Keep it clean and disconnected from the Internet as much as possible!

Download Patches

Thieves and virus gurus are always looking for new ways to infiltrate or destroy your personal computer. At the same time, the manufacturer of the computer's operating system (for example, Microsoft) is creating solutions and writing computer codes to solve the problem or "patch the hole(s)." Practically every morning when I turn on my computer a little message pops up in the bottom right-hand side of my computer screen. It says, "Updates are ready for your computer. Click here to install these updates."

All you have to do to receive these free updates is to click on the box and download the patches.

Other software programs, in addition to your computer operating system, also offer patches for problems that have been discovered within their software. Some are security related while others simply repair a problem with the software. For example, it is possible that when a new version of software is released, it won't work with certain printers. This problem can be solved by downloading the software patch or upgrade.

Wipe Clean Your Computer

No, I am not talking about keeping the dust off the top of your computer or cleaning your monitor screen. Instead, before you dispose of (trash, sell, or give away) any computer, use "wipe clean software" to erase your hard disk. And you should consider using a "wipe clean" program for deleted files—even if you are not disposing of your computer.

Some people do not realize that even when you delete a file, it remains on the computer in your "recycle bin." If you don't believe me, check it out right now. Go to your computer desktop; this is the screen that usually appears when you first turn on your computer each day. Look for the "icon" on your screen that says "Recycle Bin" (on a PC system) or "Trash" (on a Macintosh computer). It usually looks like a trash can.

Take your mouse and left double-click on the recycle bin. Surprise! All those files you thought you had deleted are still on your computer. To empty the recycle bin, click on "empty recycle bin" (or "empty trash"). Now all the files in the recycle bin have disappeared.

But have they really been removed from your computer? Surprise again! The real answer is no. Even at this point, with special software these deleted files can be restored to your computer. *Now that's really frightening.* All your deleted financial data, all your deleted love letters, all your deleted personal journal notes can be retrieved off your old discarded computer by someone with the right software.

Many years ago I sold an old computer (with all the files deleted) at a yard sale at my house. Later on that day the individual who purchased the old computer showed up again at the yard sale and made a comment about some data he found on the computer. What he said was nothing alarming, but it was an event that I will never forget.

Maybe you are breaking out into a cold sweat right about now thinking about who might have access to your personal data. Well, the truth is that most people will never go to the trouble retrieving your deleted data on that old discarded computer. However, you do need to be concerned—it can happen. You need to begin using "Wipe Clean" software to *really* delete those files, especially when you discard your old computer.

Have you ever heard the term "format a disk" or "format your computer"? When you format a floppy disk, CD, or the hard disk drive in your computer, you are restoring it to "new or clean state." You are erasing all the data and reprogramming it for a fresh start.

Most people believe that when they "format" a disk, CD, or their computer, all the data is erased. This is not always the case. People with the right software can recover data even after a disk has been formatted.

PROTECTING YOURSELF ON THE INTERNET: THE BASICS

The Internet has become the vehicle we often use to remain connected to the world. We use the Internet to communicate through e-mails; to do research; to access newspapers; to view Web sites; and to make purchases and perform financial transactions, just to name a few.

In order to fully understand the danger of using the Internet, you need to understand a few basic facts about the Internet.

The Internet Connection

There are three basic ways to connect to the Internet: (1) dial-up, using a telephone line; (2) broadband, using either a DSL or cable connection; and (3) wireless, using a radio frequency.

Most people who use a phone line for a dial-up connection get on the Internet and when finished hit the disconnect key. That's an excellent practice.

In the investment world, there is a saying: "The greater your level of risk, the greater your potential for gain or loss." Here is a saying in the Internet world: "The less time on the Internet, the lower your potential for risk." This does not mean you have no risk, but the level of risk is lower. However, most people who use a broadband or wireless connection remain connected for hours, even nonstop for days. Why? See the Hot Tip "For Non-Tech Iternet Users" for both an explanation and a suggestion to improve Internet security.

FOR NON-TECH INTERNET USERS

Let me clear up one point here for the "non-tech" Internet users (or computer dummies). Just because your phone line is connected to your computer does not mean you are "connected" to the Internet or "online." In order to be connected (or online), you must first "dial up" and "log on" to the Internet. When you finish your work, you should log off the Internet, which also disconnects the phone call (even though the phone line is still plugged into the back of your computer).

However, if you connect through your cable company or DSL (special phone line), you could be online 24 hours a day (24/7). Even when you use DSL or cable Internet connection, you can disconnect when you are not using the Internet. Most just leave the computer online because it is convenient and it does not cost any more.

Downloading Files

Don't download files unless you know exactly whom they are from. Never download a file from a stranger or unsolicited e-mail. If you open this file, it could contain a virus or spyware, or the file could hijack your computer and modem for fraudulent activities.

Downloading Free Software

Not all free software on the Internet can be dangerous, but when downloaded some can come with spyware. You thought you were downloading fifty free computer games off the Internet! Well, you did download fifty free computer games, PLUS one spyware software package. You just did not know the spyware was part of the deal!

Terms You Should Know

SPYWARE

Spyware is software that secretly gathers user information (while on the Internet) without the user's knowledge. Spyware software is typically loaded onto your computer as a hidden component in free software programs downloaded from the Internet. Once installed on your computer system, the software begins to monitor your activity and send that information to someone while you are on the Internet. Information about your e-mail addresses, credit cards, passwords, and personal data can be obtained and transmitted.

If your computer has been running "sluggish" lately, it's possible you have been infected with spyware or a computer virus. Have a computer tech scan your computer for spyware or a virus.

Use of Passwords

One of the best security features on the Internet is the use of a *password*. It's a unique combination of letters and numbers (occasionally all numbers) that you choose in order to gain exclusive entry into your account. Typically you need a password and a user ID to access personal information. If the password is incorrect (either you mistype it or forget it), you will be asked to type it again, correctly. After a few more incorrect attempts, you will be locked out and asked to contact the company (at a toll-free number) or to answer a personal question; answer your personal security question correctly, and the company will e-mail the correct password to you.

All this security is great—it helps protect your data from intruders. Clearly passwords are important, so in creating and maintaining them, there are some things you should do.

When you create passwords, use a combination of upper and lower case letters, plus numbers, with a minimum of six to eight characters. Another good rule is to avoid using words you will find in a dictionary. Think of a phrase that will help you remember your password, such as, "I love chocolate chip cookies." Your password would become "Ilccc". You might develop a code for your level of password security. For example, for very important confidential and financial information you could add the number 100 to your password, symbolizing a maximum level of security. You could use the number 1 for nonconfidential, nonfinancial passwords. Therefore, when you are setting up a password for your Internet banking, the password might be "Ilccc100." A nonfinancial password that you might use to log in to a newspaper Web site might be "Ilccc1".

It's also important to remember not to set up and use the same password for every account. And it's best to change your password frequently. Some experts recommend you change your passwords at least once every thirty days. Using the same password month after month and year after year will put you in a higher-risk category for your identity to be stolen!

Never tape your passwords on your computer! The best advice: Memorize them or use some type of a "secret code" to help you remember.

Automatic Log-In

For personal, confidential, or financial Web sites, never use the automatic log-in feature that saves your log-in name and password. I repeat, never use the automatic log-in feature!

It might save you a few seconds when you log on, but the level of risk is too great for you to be using this time-saving feature.

MORE WAYS OF PROTECTING YOURSELF ON THE INTERNET

These are the basics of Internet security. But there's much more to do to protect yourself on the Internet.

Logging Out

Every time you log on to an online account (bank, brokerage, etc.) you need to be sure you terminate your connection by clicking the "log out" link on the site. Don't just close the browser. You need to log out. This is like locking the back door when you are leaving. Otherwise the door is still open, and others might be able to view your account without your knowledge, by simply reopening the Web site on your computer (or worse, on a public computer).

Terms You Should Know

HACKER

Someone who achieves unauthorized access to a computer or computer network. A hacker uses a series of attempts (most failing) until he/she is able to break into the system. They just keep "hacking away" on their keyboard until they find a way to enter a computer system they are not authorized to enter.

Key Chain Fob

If you have not heard about this one—you will. It's called a key fob, and it's already being used by some online brokerage houses. This is how it works. After you type in your user name and password, you look at your key chain fob and type in a six-digit code found on a tiny screen. Here's the exciting part: This key fob code usually changes every sixty seconds—so no crook will ever be able to know the current code to enter your account. It's like being issued a new password every sixty seconds!

At this writing, 99 percent of all financial institutions require only your user name and password to access your account. Federal regulators have mandated financial institutions to tighten security systems before the end of 2006. Keep watching for more key chain fobs to be showing up. When your financial institution begins to offer a key chain fob for password security—use it!

Delete Temporary Internet Files

Try to avoid using a computer that does not belong to you when viewing brokerage or bank accounts online. For example, do not use a computer at the public library to check your bank account information. However, if you have to use a computer that does not belong to you, once you log out, do the following to clear all the temporary Internet files and history from the browser after you are finished. For Microsoft Internet Explorer, you can accomplish this by clicking on the *Tools* menu, select *Internet Options*, then select *Delete Files* from the *temporary Internet files* area and *Clear History* from the *History* area.

Although you must follow this procedure if you are using a computer that belongs to someone else, you should also be deleting temporary Internet files on your own personal computer—especially if other people have access to your computer.

Hot Spots

A hot spot is an area where you can log on to the Internet with a wireless connection. Currently the most common areas for hot spots are places like office buildings, libraries, and coffee shops. As I documented in my book *Cashing It In*, one day we will have a global hot spot. You will be able to connect to the Internet from anywhere in the world to receive e-mails, visit Web sites, and make financial transactions!

Here is my advice about wireless connections: Try to avoid logging on to financial sites when using wireless Internet in coffee shops, airports, or hotels. It is possible for a thief to intercept your data. If you have to connect wireless, be sure your "wireless ad hoc mode" is disabled. (Fortunately, most laptops already come with the ad hoc mode disabled.) This will not allow your computer to find and communicate with other wireless devices in the hot spot area.

E-Mail

The first thing you need to understand about regular e-mail accounts is that *they are not secure*. Information you include in a regular e-mail letter has the potential to be viewed by numerous sets of eyes.

Before we talk about the most common way to steal someone's identity using e-mail, here's a list of some general guidelines for using e-mail:

- Never open e-mail file attachments sent to you by strangers. They have a high level of risk and might contain a computer virus. In fact, you should even be cautious opening file attachments from people you know.

- Never click on links in e-mail unless you know the person providing the link and know that it does not relate to financial data. For example, it would be okay to send a friend a link in an e-mail to an article in a newspaper or a great Web site.

- Never send personal data such as credit card numbers in an e-mail. For example, let's say your son (in college) needs to make a major purchase online. Don't e-mail him your credit card information! Call on a land-line phone (mobile-phone calls at times can be intercepted) and give him the number.

- Never send any confidential information that you would not want someone else to read through e-mail.

Many computer problems, including complete shutdown or a very slow-running machine, are the result of an e-mail that contained a computer virus.

Next, let's talk about a popular e-mail scam called phishing. We all know what it's like to go fishing. You bait several hooks, drop them into the water, and wait for a stupid fish to eat the bait. Well, e-mail phishing is similar. An e-mail—sent by would be thieves—arrives asking you to update an acount within twenty-four hours, providing you with a link to do so.

Terms You Should Know

PHISHING (PRONOUNCED *FISHING*)

Phishing is a scam in which thieves send out an official-looking e-mail requesting a response that discloses personal information. The thieves send out thousands of those e-mails—often complete with a recognized logo—in hopes you will bite on the bait. The e-mail informs the recipient that unless she clicks on the link below and updates the account within twenty-four hours, the account will be closed. (This was discussed in Scam #1.) They are "phishing" for personal data to open a credit card account under your name and stick you with the bill.

Those who click the link will go to an official looking form that contains blanks for your name, address, birth date, telephone numbers, and Social Security number. Complete those blanks, and the thief has everything he/she needs to begin opening credit card accounts under your name and going on a spending spree. The thief may also use the data to get a personal loan at a bank or otherwise use your identity for personal or financial gain.

If you receive a suspicious e-mail and wonder if it is "phishy," look for some of the following things that "might" signal FRAUD.

- The e-mail has an official looking credit card or bank logo.

- The wording sounds like "this is official business."

- The e-mail contains phrases or sentences such as, "Urgent response is necessary," or . . .

"We regret to inform you that your account is about to be closed."

"Your account will become inactive in seven days if you do not update your information."

"We have temporarily limited access to your account."

"We have received your order for $_____ and have charged your account. If you did not place this order, click on the 'dispute' link below."

"To avoid problems with your account, please click on the link below and reenter your data to be sure your account has been updated."

"According to Section 9 of our agreement, you are required to annually update your account data. Please click on the secure Web site link below."

"Our fraud department has determined that your credit cards are at risk. You must click on the link below to confirm and update your data, or all your credit cards will become inactive in 24 hours (for your safety)."

Don't take the bait. Know the "warning signals" for an e-mail scam. These crooks are phishing for your personal data. Remember the Action Alert in chapter 1: *No financial institution or law enforcement agency will ever call you and ask you to provide personal data* on the phone. If you receive an e-mail or phone call asking you to give or verify personal data—it's a scam! Delete the e-mail or hang up the phone and report it to the Federal Trade Commission: www.ftc.gov.

Bogus Web Sites

It's not as common as phishing, but another scam you
need to be aware of is what is called pharming (see
above). The best way to visit a Web site is to type in the
Web address yourself—not by clicking on a link. Thieves
who "pharm" hope you will take their shortcut, which is
actually a detour that redirects you to the criminal's
phony Web site where he can glean the "fruit" of your
personal data.

Look for Signs of a Secure Web Site

A secure Web site will have a small yellow padlock symbol
at the bottom of your computer screen. It's a little "lock"
icon. This symbol is one indication that the site is secure.

Also look and see if the URL for the Web site begins
with "https." The *s* stands for secure. For example, it
might say: https://www.firstbank.com.

If the Web site uses encryption to hide your actual
Social Security number and other private data, it will
have this "lock" icon or "https." If it has the "lock" icon
or "https," is the site 100 percent secure? Well, not 100
percent secure, but at least 99.9 percent. Crooks have
even found ways to forge security icons.

Pop-Ups

How many times have you been on the Internet and some type of a Pop-up ad suddenly appears? In some cases they are offering free software. The most cautious approach would be to never download software from a pop-up ad. It's *much too risky*.

Another common pop-up that I have seen says:

> *"WARNING: Your computer may be infected with harmful spyware programs or viruses. Immediate removal may be required. To scan your computer click 'YES' below."*

My advice is that you never—repeat, *never*—accept their "gracious" offer. Don't hit the "scan now" or the "yes" button; in fact, don't even hit the "no, thanks" or "cancel" button. Just click on the red box with an "X" usually in the top right-hand corner, which will safely remove the message. Probably the only thing this "free scan" will offer is a free virus or spyware onto your computer! Scan your own computer with your own antivirus software!

Cookie

Every time you visit a Web site, it has the potential to deposit what is known as a *cookie* into your computer. Cookies enables the site to gather information to personalize the page and customize it for your ease of use. However, unless you restrict the use of cookies, the Web site also can send such information about you to marketers—like what Web sites you have visited—which tells them what interests you.

Terms You Should Know

COOKIE

"The main purpose of cookies is to identify users and possibly prepare customized Web pages for them. When you enter a Web site using cookies, you may be asked to fill out a form providing such information as your name and interests. This information is packaged into a cookie and sent to your Web browser which stores it for later use. The next time you go to the same Web site, your browser will send the cookie to the Web server. The server can use this information to present you with custom Web pages. So, for example, instead of seeing just a generic welcome page you might see a welcome page with your name on it."

Source: www.webopedia.com

Have you ever visited a Web site that sells books? Ever done a search for a book by subject? Ever bought a book on a Web site? Well, I have. Every time I return to that site an ad might pop up that says, "You might be interested in these books." Why are most of them Christian books? Because that is what I have expressed interest in. Do you think they have a pop-up of Christian books for everyone? No way!

Hunters have sports books pop up!

NASCAR fans have racing books pop up!

That doesn't happen just by accident! That cookie makes it happen.

In addition, on certain Web sites cookies may be deposited into your computer without your filling out a form! How do you protect against abuses through cookies? The answer is, know your Web site. Read their "Terms of Use" or privacy policy to learn whether they gather cookies and, if so, how they use them. If they don't mention the practice—or they don't offer terms of use—it may not be worth using the site.

Unsubscribe Link

Don't ever click on the "unsubscribe" link on an e-mail message you receive, unless you previously signed up for a subscription or you know for certain that the company is legitimate.

Have you ever received an unsolicited e-mail from a company that you knew nothing about and did not want to know anything about? We all have. How many times have you clicked on the "unsubscribe link" at the bottom? You know the line—"Click here to unsubscribe," or, "Click here to remove your name from our mailing list."

Baloney! It might as well read, "All fools click here." Don't do it unless you know it is a legitimate company.

Why? Here is what e-mail spammers do. They do not know your valid address; therefore, they send out millions of e-mails trying to find valid e-mail addresses. For example, they might send out the following e-mails:

johnsmith@e-mailnet.com
john@e-mailnet.com
jsmith@e-mailnet.com
js@e-mailnet.com
josmith@e-mailnet.com
john@e-mailnet.com
johns@e-mailnet.com
jn@e-mailnet.com

Your correct address is js@e-mailnet.com. All the rest of the e-mails bounce back, and the good address arrives in your e-mail box.

You receive the unwanted e-mail, see "unsubscribe" or "remove from list" on the bottom of the e-mail, and click on it. They receive your response, and now they know that js@e-mailnet.com is valid and sell your "validated" address and thousands of others to companies to use for marketing!

ACTION ALERT

TALK TO YOUR KIDS

There is a good chance that your children are spending more time on the computer and Internet than you are.

Do you think they know about "phishing"? How about the danger in downloading files? How to handle bogus e-mails? Spyware? The danger in downloading free software onto the family computer?

Sit down and go over the things you have learned in this book about computers and the Internet. Maybe you are careful when using the Internet, but your kids could be putting the personal data on your computer at risk by making some poor decisions while online—and you didn't even know it.

More Prevention

HOW CAN YOU PROTECT YOUR CHECKING ACCOUNT, CREDIT CARDS, AND OTHER PERSONAL INFORMATION?

WE'VE LOOKED AT PHISHING and pharming, dumpster diving and hacking. But there are less exotic yet equally dangerous ways your identity is at risk.

In this chapter we will look at how unguarded documents and correspondence, including our checking accounts and everyday mail, can make us vulnerable to ID theft—and how we should respond.

In fact, we will look at eleven more "bricks" that will add to "Your Wall of Protection" (see next page). We begin with key ways to protect yourself while writing checks.

Your Wall of Protection

ID Insurance	Avoiding Scams	Action Alerts	Being on Alert
Your Statements	Credit Cards	Unsolicited Mail	Credit Reports
While Traveling	On Telephone	Your Investments	In Public Places
Writing Checks	ID Cards	Applications	U.S. Mail
At Home	At Work	Your Computer	On the Internet

PROTECTING YOUR BANK CHECKS

As I documented in my book *Cashing It In*, the use of personal checks peaked in the mid-1990s and is decreasing at a rate of 4 percent annually. But while we are still using checks, there are some things you never want to do with your personal checks—and some things you must do to protect your personal identity.

Avoid Showing Your Social Security Number on Checks

Never print your Social Security number on your check! Recently a friend of mine, Greg (not his real name), sent a financial contribution to our ministry. Later, as I looked at the check, to my surprise, his *and* his wife's Social Security numbers were printed on the check. *Whoa!* Red Alert! Red Alert! Red Alert!

When I saw Greg later, I smiled, put my hand on his shoulder, issued him a mild rebuke, and strongly encouraged him to remove the Social Security numbers from his checks . . . tomorrow! We even had a good laugh about it.

The same thing had happened with another friend several months earlier. I gave him a similar mild rebuke on the phone.

Printing your name, address, phone number, *and Social Security number* on your check is giving someone almost everything they need to steal your identity, open up fraudulent accounts in your name, and go on a major spending spree—all on your good name. Don't make it easier for a thief by printing it in bold on your check!

If you have your Social Security number printed on your check, spend a few dollars and order some new checks today! And before the new checks arrive, take a bold black pen and cover up your Social Security number on any check you write.

Use an Initial for Your First Name

One banker I know has recommended that his customers consider printing their first initial and last name on their checks. For example, I could print E. Pope on my checks. When a person sees E. Pope they will not immediately be able to determine if I am a man or a woman. You would also need to begin signing your checks with your first initial and last name. This lack of information and "hassle" just might be enough for a potential bandit to move on to someone else.

Avoid Printing Your Home Phone Number

If someone has your phone number, he or she can find your address. Your physical address and phone numbers are very useful information for anyone attempting to steal your identity. Anyone can go to www.whitepages. com and type in a phone number and find out the owner's name and physical address! *Just to see how easy it is—go ahead and try it right now—enter* www.whitepages.com. Look for the "REVERSE PHONE" link at the top of the page, type in your phone number, and see what happens! You will even find a map providing directions to your home.

In light of this information being available on the Internet, you might consider printing a work phone number on your checks if you believe a contact phone number is necessary.

Use a P.O. Box on Your Checks

If possible, begin using a post office box on your checks. The less personal information you provide on your printed checks, the harder it becomes for someone to steal your identity. Using a P.O. box makes it harder for someone to find important data about you. Using a physical address tells them where you live, your phone number, and where your mail is delivered each day.

Be Careful Filling in the Memo Line

Don't write your credit card number on the memo line when you pay your bill. *I know, I know.* All the credit card companies tell you to put your credit card number on the memo line when you are making a payment. In my opinion, too many eyes view my check. For over twenty-five years I have never written my credit card number on the memo line. I recommend that you don't do it either.

Terms You Should Know

DEBIT CARD

A debit card, sometimes known as a check card, is linked directly to your checking account. When you make a purchase and use a debit card, the money is immediately (or later in the day) transferred out of your checking account. At the end of each month, your debit purchases will be documented on your bank statement (just like your checks are). Be on the alert, though. Just because the transaction goes through does not always mean there is enough money in your account to cover the transaction. Be sure you have enough in your account, or your bank will charge an overdraft fee—just like when you write a physical check!

CREDIT CARD

When you make a purchase and use a credit card, the amount of your purchase goes onto your credit card account. At the end of the month, you are mailed a credit card statement documenting all of your charges. You have the option to pay the bill in full or in part. You can use a credit card and make purchases even if you don't have the money in your bank account to pay for your purchase. Credit cards are extending you a line of credit up to a pre-approved amount. Of course, you must repay every dollar of credit. Because of interest that the credit card company charges, it make sense to pay off the balance as soon as possible.

Start Using a Debit Card

When you pay for your purchase with a debit card, it's just like writing a check—except easier and more secure. Just think about it. The transaction is processed electronically—with fewer eyes viewing the data. It takes less time—no standing there writing out the check. No identification is required, no having to pull out your driver's licenses, and no cashier looking at your personal data and writing phone numbers and ID numbers on the face of your check.

PROTECTING YOUR IDENTIFICATION CARDS

Change Your Driver's License Number

Many states use the person's Social Security number as the driver's license number. If this is true for your state, you should change the number immediately. If you ask, most states will allow you to stop using your Social Security number and obtain a unique driver's license number. I did this about five years ago. *Remind other members of your family to do the same.*

You might be asking, Why change your number? Just think about how many times you are asked to provide your driver's license for identification. Typically whenever you write a check, the vendor writes your driver's license number (Social Security number) and birth date on your check. Numerous people will view your check and your Social Security number—the sales clerk, the person making the deposit, the bank teller and bank proofers, and so forth.

Finding and using a person's Social Security number is the primary ingredient used to steal your identity and your good name.

Safely Store Your Social Security Card

Never, never carry your Social Security card in your wallet or purse. Keep it located in a secure location. Your original Social Security card in the hands of a thief will create nothing but trouble.

Use of Social Security Number

Businesses may request your Social Security number in order to transact business; there is no federal law, however, requiring that you provide it. Your only option, if you don't want to provide it, is to walk out the door and forget the transaction.

Banks and financial institutions (like mutual fund companies) are required by federal law to obtain your Social Security number. Not only is this one aspect of what is known as the "Patriot Act" (post-9/11 security measures), but banks and employers also need it in order to report your income, interest earned, and any other tax-related transactions.

BEFORE YOU GIVE YOUR NUMBER

If you are asked to provide your Social Security number, be sure to ask the following four questions:

1. Why do you need my SS number?
2. How will it be used?
3. What is your privacy policy?
4. Is it required to do business?

PROTECTING YOURSELF ON APPLICATIONS

No SS Number on Résumé

You will complete many applications during your life. Very few will require that you disclose your Social Security number. Because a job résumé can lead to completing a job application, some résumé writers like to include the Social Security number. Indeed, it was common years ago to put one's name, address, telephone number, and Social Security number on the résumé. Well, times have changed; you should *never* print your Social Security number on any résumé. If you obtain the job, you will be able to provide that important information later to the human resources department.

Web Site Résumé

Never post your resume with your Social Security number on an Internet Web site. Many more eyes may be able to view your SS number, not just a couple of human resources representatives, over an insecure Web site.

Be Careful with Job Applications

If the job application requests your Social Security number, be sure to ask why they need that information. Some companies need it to run a credit check, while other companies do not need it unless they decide to hire you. Many job applications request it, just because it's been on the form for the last forty years. Unless they indicate a true need, offer to provide it once you're hired.

Credit Card and Loan Applications

You will be required to provide your Social Security number on credit card and loan applications since they need this number to check your credit report. This is a reasonable request; be sure, though, not to send the information via the Internet (unless you know it is a secure Web site) or in an e-mail response. Use the U.S. Mail or, when possible, deliver the application in person.

PROTECTING YOUR MAIL

Use Secure Mail Locations

At work, do you have an open box or basket that you can drop work and personal mail in? How about your home? Do you place your mail in a mailbox and then drive off to work? *How secure is that?*

If you place outgoing mail in an unsecured location (at home or work), thieves have the potential to steal credit card payments or personal bank data and numbers.

Here is one you probably have not thought of . . . What if a person steals your credit card payment from the mailbox, opens the letter, fills out the change of address to a bogus street address, and then proceeds to mail your check and change of address to the credit card company?

You might be thinking, *Why would they do that?* Well, by submitting a change of address they have created six to eight weeks of time to make fraudulent purchases. Because they mailed your current check, this month's bill will be paid. However, for the next four to eight weeks, your legitimate purchases *and their fraudulent purchases* will be on a credit card bill being mailed to a bogus address. Before you or the credit card company figures out what has happened, they have moved on to another victim. In other words, if you don't know about the fraudulent charges, you can't report them.

Until recently, I never really considered the level of risk we are exposing ourselves to by using "unsecured" mail service. As you can tell, I am not talking about how the U.S. Postal Service processes mail. I am focusing on what can happen to the mail *before* the U.S. Postal Service picks up the mail from an unsecured site or *after* they deliver the mail to an unsecured site.

If your mail is delivered to your home, a thief has the potential to remove mail from your mailbox before you arrive home from work. They might remove your credit card statement in order to secure your credit card number. They might remove your bank statement to secure your banking information.

For maximum security, you might consider renting a post office box from the post office and discontinue using the mailbox attached to your house or out next to the street. If you don't believe people steal mail out of unsecured mailboxes, think again. Just a few years ago I mailed a check to my local plumber, whose name began with a capital *S*. When the check arrived, the thief stole the envelope and then changed the payable line to read "Steak Out Restaurant." Later he called in an order and presented the check for payment. The cashier was suspicious and went to find her manager. By the time she returned, the thief had fled.

Install a Secure Mailbox

One alternative to renting a P.O. box from the U.S. Postal Service is to install a mailbox with a lock at your home. The mail carrier can slip the mail in the slot, and when you arrive home, you can take a key, unlock the box, and remove the mail. *Employers should also consider providing a secure mail drop box.*

When Traveling: Hold Mail

When you leave home for a few days, be sure to put a "hold" on your mail with the post office. Your local post office will store your mail for free each day you're away from home. You don't want mail to be noticeably overflowing in the mailbox attached to your front door or in your front yard. This is almost like putting a neon sign in your front yard announcing to the world, *"I am out of town for a few days. Here is your invitation to steal my mail or break into my home."*

When Traveling: Inform a Trusted Neighbor

Assuming you have neighbors you can trust, be sure you tell them that you have plans to be out of town for the next few days or weeks. When we leave town for a few days, I always laugh and tell my neighbor, "If you see anyone moving furniture out of my house, call the police." I have also asked my neighbor to watch for UPS or FedEx packages that might be left next to our front door. A package sitting next to your front door for days is another sign no one is at home.

In addition, I like to set light timers in my house so that lights will go off and on during the evening.

PROTECTING YOURSELF WHEN YOU TRAVEL

Closely related to protecting your identity at home is protecting yourself when you travel. Whether it's business or vacation travel, prepare the right way.

Clean Out Your Wallet or Purse

Before you leave, be sure you clean out your wallet of all unnecessary credit cards, identification cards, and information. Never carry your Social Security card in your wallet. Always keep it in a secure location.

Consider Using Prepaid Cards

Major credit card companies offer prepaid cards, also called gift cards. No matter what they call them, they are great to travel with. Why? These cards are not linked directly to your bank or credit card account. Some of the cards can be "reloaded" while others can be "loaded" only once. They are usually accepted anywhere debit cards and credit cards are accepted. Let's say you have a card loaded with $500. You can use this card to purchase gasoline, ice cream, and pay for meals—as long as you have money remaining on the card. You can also withdraw cash from an ATM if you need it. In addition, the card issuer will replace the money if the card is stolen. It's a great way to travel without cash.

It's also a great way to keep you from overspending. When the money runs out, you have to go home!

Hotel Rooms and Keys

When staying in a hotel room, be sure you don't leave papers, receipts, wallet, purse, or your laptop on the desk when you leave the room. It just might be too tempting for a housekeeper to write down your credit card number or see personal data.

One financial writer recommends that you take your hotel key card with you upon checkout. This applies only to card keys, not physical keys. Her article recommends you leave the card neither in the room nor at the front desk when you check out. Some hotels embed personal data (your name and other data, for example) in the magnetic strip on the back of the card.[1] That's data an identity theft may be able to use.

PROTECTING YOURSELF ON THE TELEPHONE

Never Provide Personal Data

A few weeks before my son began his freshman year in college, he received a phone call. The person calling said something like this: "Hi, Austin. Congratulations on being accepted to the University of Florida. We need to confirm some information. Do you have a few minutes? First, we need to verify your permanent mailing address, date of birth, and Social Security number."

Alert! Alert! went off in Austin's brain. Austin recognized the threat and refused to provide his personal data. He simply hung up the phone. **Great job, Austin!**

Remember the caution in chapter 1, scam #2: *No legitimate institution (university, police, bank, business, credit card company) will ever call you on the phone and ask for personal data,* such as your Social Security number. Once you determine this is not a legitimate phone call, it's OK to be "rude" and *hang up on a scammer*!

Don't Fall for the Free Vacation

Just after dinner one night I received a phone call. The person on the phone said, "You have been selected to receive a free ten-day vacation." I said, "Great!" Then she said, "Mr. Pope, all I need for you to do in order for me to reserve your vacation package is cover the $9.95 handling fee. Which credit card would you like to put this on?" My immediate response was, "I thought you said it was free! No thanks." Click.

What's the scam here? The caller was not looking to trick me out of $9.95, but to trick me into giving him my credit card number and the three- or four-number security code printed on the back or front of my credit card. Be assured, their intentions as con artists far exceeded scamming me for a minuscule $9.95.

PROTECTING YOUR INVESTMENTS

Online Brokerage Accounts

Many investment firms provide the convenience of immediate access to information as well as the ability to perform financial transactions online. Here are some important things to remember when you are using a brokerage Web site (indeed, any financial Web site): (1) Always use a strong password; (2) change your password frequently; and (3) check to make sure the Web site is secure (a lock icon appears and *https* shows on the address line). In addition, when you are finished always "log off" the Web site.

Government Approval

According to the Securities and Exchange Commission's Web site (www.sec.gov), the government does not "endorse" any investment. With computer technology, it's relatively easy for a thief to cut and paste official looking seals on investment documents or on Web sites and imply this investment is "approved by the SEC."

In a variation of this scam, a scammer says he has the phone number for the Securities and Exchange Commission and recommends you call the SEC to check out the company. When you make the call, the scammer's friend sitting in the next office answers the phone, "Hello this is the SEC, and how may I help you?" Remember, the SEC will not recommend a company or give advice over the phone. If you are calling *any* office to verify information, look up the number yourself, and then make the call.

Know the Company

Be very careful in dealing with companies you have never heard of, especially if they are located out of state. Here are two helpful Web sites to check out companies: www.nasd.com and www.sec.gov.

PROTECTING YOURSELF IN PUBLIC PLACES

Guard the Keypad

Let me warn you to be a little more on guard when transacting business in a public place. Be cautious when you are in the checkout line, using an ATM machine, or the U-Scan lane in the grocery store. If you are required to input a PIN or code, be sure to cover the keypad with your other hand.

One banker I know recommends that when a cashier asks you, "Debit or credit?" always say, "Credit," even if you are using a debit card. The money will still be taken out of your checking account that day as a debit transaction, but you will be asked to sign your name instead of putting in a pin number. Why is this important? If you ever have to challenge a purchase, you will be able to see your signature. This is one way to prove that someone else made the purchase. *What a great recommendation!*

Terms You Should Know

SHOULDER-SURFING

Someone is standing close by in line—almost to your shoulder. Why? He's trying to hear or read your credit card number and four-digit security code. Sometimes a shoulder-surfer will try to see you type your user name and password into the computer.

Speak Softly

When talking on the phone in a public place like a store or office, speak softly when providing personal data. You don't want the person next to you to be able to hear your credit card number and security code.

PROTECTING YOUR FINANCIAL STATEMENTS

According to the FTC, "The most common way victims discovered the misuse of their personal information was by monitoring the activity in their accounts. This includes examining monthly statements from banks and credit card issuers. 52% of all victims cited this as the way they first found out they were victims of Identity Theft."[2]

As the chart below shows, the other common way victims learned of account fraud was through receiving notification by their bank or credit card company because of suspicious activity (26 percent). Some found out they were victims because they had lost their wallet or were victims of theft (9 percent) or they had been turned down for credit (8 percent).

HOW VICTIMS DISCOVERED ID THEFT

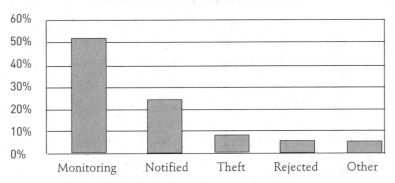

SOURCE: Federal Trade Commission, "Identity Theft Survey Report," September 2003, 39.

What is the lesson we can learn from these statistics? Monitor your account, reconcile your bank statement, and evaluate your credit card statements carefully.

Reconcile Your Bank Statement

Be sure you take the time to reconcile and review your bank statement every month.

While my mother was alive, I began helping her reconcile her bank statement each month. One month I noticed an electronic transfer for about $200 on her bank statement. I later discovered that it had not been an approved transfer. After making a few phone calls and investigating the transfer, I determined that it was fraudulent. Someone had obtained her bank account number and initiated an electronic transfer out of her account.

If I (or someone else) had not been reviewing and reconciling her bank statement each month, this transfer would have gone unnoticed, due to her failing eyesight and inability to reconcile her bank statement. If the thief saw that he or she got away with it once, you can be assured more unauthorized transfers would take place in the future.

Let me ask you a question. Unless you reconcile your bank statement each month, how do you know this has not been happening over the last few months to you or a family member? *The fact is you don't! Alert, alert, alert!*

Review Your Credit Card Statements

Be sure you carefully examine your credit card statements every month. Just as important as reconciling your bank statement each month, you need to carefully review each credit card statement.

How do you do this? Whenever I make a credit card purchase, I always put the receipt in one place: my wallet. My wife keeps all her receipts in her purse. At the end of each week, I place all my credit card receipts in my credit card folder. When the bill arrives, I look at each item on the statement and find the corresponding receipt in my file. When I find the receipt, I place a check next to the amount on the credit card statement. If I cannot find the receipt, I do more investigating. It is possible I lost a receipt, but very unlikely. Next, I check my calendar to see if this would help me remember making a charge at a specific restaurant or gas station. If I cannot find any documentation of my charge, I then call the credit card company and ask them to research the charge and provide me the proper documentation.

Without reviewing your credit card statement, how do you know that someone isn't making a purchase each month using your credit card number? *The fact is you don't. Alert, alert, alert!*

In addition, if your credit card bill does not arrive as scheduled, call the credit card company's customer service immediately. All credit cards have a toll-free customer service number printed on the back of the card. If the bill did not arrive on schedule, it is possible someone requested a change of address for your account. You might be asking, "So what?" It's a *big "so what,"* because the thief has bought several weeks of time to make more purchases before you know unauthorized charges are being made.

PROTECTING YOUR CREDIT CARDS

Protect Your Security Code

The four numbers printed on the front or the three numbers on the back of your credit card are part of a relatively new security code being used by credit card companies. It's really a great system compared to the old system. When placing an order on the phone or Internet, not only do you need the credit card number, but you also need the security code. Another level of security is they ask for the zip code your statement is mailed to. In my opinion, the more questions or levels of security to approve a charge, the better.

Never Sign the Back of Your Credit Card

I know what you are thinking: "But it says on the back, 'Authorized Signature—not valid unless signed.'" Yes, but if you sign it, you give a would-be forger the perfect model he needs to make a copy. The best thing to write on the back of your credit card is "Photo ID Required."

Limit the Number of Credit Cards

Try to use one or two credit cards at the most. The fewer cards you have, the lower your risk of identity theft or fraud. In addition, the fewer you have to monitor and keep up with, the better.

Terms You Should Know

SKIMMING

Your card is "skimmed" when a thief captures your account number and PIN without stealing your card. The numbers are captured when you run your card through a card reader that a trickster has attached over the actual card reader at an ATM machine, for example. If the card scanner looks weird, different, or added on, don't use it.

Maintain Low Limits

How much do you really need for your credit card limit? Credit card companies on occasion will increase your credit limit without you even asking. Before you know it, your limit could become $20,000. If your monthly credit card bill is always around $700 and has been for the last five years, why do you need to have a credit limit of $20,000? Consider decreasing it to $2,500 or less. Why would you do this? Well, it will keep a thief from being able to run up $20,000 of charges on your account.

However, if you are planning to purchase a home or car using debt, your credit report will be evaluated. As long as your credit card balance is 60 percent or lower than your limit, your credit score is not negatively impacted. If your balance is consistently over 60 percent of your credit limit, *even though you pay your credit card bill in full every month*, you might lose several points on your credit score. If you are obtaining a loan or credit card, the better your credit report score, the lower the interest rate you will be offered.

Use One Credit Card for Online Purchases

Another thing you can do is to use one credit card (with a low credit limit) for all online purchases. Then if someone steals your number, they won't be able to have too much fun.

Keep Receipts in a Secure Location

Once you confirm all the charges are valid on your credit card statement, you need to store your statement and receipts in a safe location. The general rule is to keep your documents for seven years. In some cases the need to keep documentation is shorter and in others it is longer. Check with your tax and financial advisors for advice.

UNSOLICITED MAIL

Opt Out of Preapproved
Credit Cards and Marketing Letters

The "You're preapproved" letters that most of us consider as junk mail are far more dangerous than you think.
Here's why. Toss them without shredding them and a
"dumpster diver" may find those letters in your garbage,
complete the applications, intercept the new card, and
charge purchases under your name. In addition, if you
sign up for several new cards, the temptation is to spend
. . . spend . . . spend. There is a way to stop most of them
from arriving in your mailbox—if you desire. Federal
law requires the opt-out phone number to be placed on
the front page of all these mailings. Here is how it looks:

ACTION ALERT

TO OPT OUT

To opt out of receiving preapproved credit card
offers:

(1) Call 888-5-OPT-OUT (888-567-8688), or
(2) go to the following Internet address on the
Web: www.optoutprescreen.com

Choosing to opt out does not guarantee you will
eliminate all preapproved offers, but it will
greatly reduce the number of solicitations in
your mailbox.

You can choose to stop receiving "prescreened" offers of credit from this and other companies by calling toll-free 1-888-5-OPT-OUT. See PRESCREEN & OPT-OUT NOTICE in the enclosed Important Disclosures for more information about prescreened offers.

Make that choice. Choose to opt out of receiving these preapproved offers. It's simple and will reduce the clutter in your mailbox and the danger in your home. See the Action Alert on page 104.

Stop Convenience Checks

How many times have you received "convenience checks" in the mail from your credit card company? You know, the ones that especially come before Christmas, April 15, or the beginning of summer. Why do you think they show up then? The credit card companies know that most people cannot control their spending at Christmas, they need money to pay their taxes, or they would love to have money for a vacation. You can be assured, they are not sending these checks because they love you; they are doing it because when millions of people use them, they make lots of money.

Contact your credit card company and ask them to stop including those "convenience" checks in the mail. See the "Convenience Checks" Action Alert on page 106 to learn how.

Convenience checks are dangerous for two reasons: (1) A thief could steal them out of your mailbox and use them to make purchases; and (2) when the preprinted checks show up, they tempt people with little or no self-control to spend money they don't have and increase their credit card debt.

ACTION ALERT

CONVENIENCE CHECKS

It's relatively quick and easy to get your credit card provider to stop offering convenience checks in the mail. Just look on the back of your credit card(s) for the customer service phone number. Then call the number and ask them to "cease delivery of convenience checks."

They will give you five reasons why you should not do this, but be firm in your request.

NOTES

1. Sandra Block, "How to Keep Your Cash, Cards and Personal Info Safe," *USA Today*, May 31, 2005; www.usatoday.com/money/perfi/columnist/block/2005-05-31-personal-info_x.htm
2. Federal Trade Commission, "Identity Theft Survey Report," September 2003, 39; www.ftc.gov/os/2003/09/synovatcreport.pdf.

Still More Prevention

WHAT OUTSIDE RESOURCES
CAN YOU USE TO PROTECT YOURSELF?

IF YOU ACT UPON ALL the recommendations of the past two chapters, you're on your way to building a solid wall of protection against identity theft. Now let's look at the final five bricks in this wall. Two of them point us to outside resources to consider; the remaining three are commonsense preventives that call upon us to have a watchful, cautious attitude. (See next page for the complete wall of protection.)

ORDERING ANNUAL CREDIT REPORTS

Be sure you schedule credit report checks on an annual basis. Federal law provides that all three credit reporting companies shall provide a report annually at no cost. I recommend you *request a credit report from one of the three companies once every four months*. This will allow you to keep tabs on your credit report at three different times during the year—compared to just once a year if you were to order all the reports at one time.

Your Wall of Protection

ID Insurance	Avoiding Scams	Action Alerts	Being on Alert
Your Statements	Credit Cards	Unsolicited Mail	Credit Reports
While Traveling	On Telephone	Your Investments	In Public Places
Writing Checks	ID Cards	Applications	U.S. Mail
At Home	At Work	Your Computer	On the Internet

The primary purpose is not to be checking your credit score, but to discover whether:

- any unauthorized accounts have been opened in your name.

- any unauthorized loans have been taken out in your name.

- any unauthorized activity has taken place in your name.

- any company or person has run a credit check on you.

- any information is not correct in your report.

How to Order Your Free Report

As noted in scam #3, there is only one Web site you use to request your free credit report. See the Action Alert on the next page; again note that *only one Web site will give you a free report.* This is important to remember, because some companies are offering "free credit reports" under misleading Web sites. When you request a free credit report from such a site, you will receive the free report, but you are also signing up for some type of identity theft insurance with a monthly or annual premium and probably don't even know you signed up for it.

Action Alert

FREE CREDIT REPORT

You cannot request your free annual credit report directly from the specific credit reporting agency. There is *only one* Web site, phone number, or address to request your report:

www.annualcreditreport.com
1-877-322-8228

Annual Credit Report Request Service
P.O. Box 105281
Atlanta, GA 30348-5281

You may obtain the "Annual Credit Report Request Form" at www.ftc.gov/credit. Then mail the form to the Atlanta address shown above.

Begin requesting your annual report once every four months!

The Process

I remember my first visit to www.annualcreditreport. com. I was actually a little nervous not knowing what to expect. I had never ordered a credit report before. Here is what you can expect to happen when you visit www. annualcreditreport.com:

1. After you enter your name, address, and Social Security number, you will indicate which credit reporting company you would like to request a credit report from. I recommend you select only one. Then in four months, visit the site again and select another company. One suggestion that will help you remember which one to order is to order them in alphabetical order. That would mean requesting Equifax in January, Experian in May, and TransUnion in September.

2. Once you hit the continue button, you will be taken to the Web site of the company you selected.

3. Next you will be asked to answer a question that *only you should know the answer to.* For example, what is the amount of your mortgage payment with ABC Bank? ❏ $100–$400; ❏ $401–$600; ❏ $601–$999; ❏ $1000 +

4. Once you clear this verification screening device, you will be taken to the next screen that asks if you would like to purchase your credit score. Federal law does not require the company to provide your score with your free report. If you want your score, you will have to pay a few dollars. I simply clicked the "No, Thanks" and went to the next screen.

5. Surprise, Surprise . . . Now they want to know if you would like to sign up for a credit monitoring service for a few bucks a month. Once again I clicked on the "No, thanks" button and went to the next screen.

6. After several more sales pitches you finally get to view and print out your credit report. Or, if there are problems with the verification question, you will receive your free credit report in the mail. Don't be concerned if this happens to you. It happened to me on my first attempt.

Your Review of the Report

Once you receive your free credit report, what are you looking for? Here are ten areas to consider as you review your credit report:

- See whether you have any active credit cards that you are not using or do not know about. If you do, call the toll-free number provided and close them immediately.

- See whether the report contains any untrue statements. If you find one and you can verify that it is indeed not true, contact the credit bureau by sending a "Request for Investigation." You can fill this out on the Web site, or if you received your credit report in the mail, a form will be included.

- See whether someone has taken a loan out in your name. It is possible that someone stole your identity, obtained a loan, provided a bogus address, and your loan is now in default—and you never even knew it.

- Verify any loan(s) by lender, and the amount of the loan(s).

- Verify that your employer is listed correctly.

- Verify your current and past addresses and phone numbers.

- Verify who has recently requested your credit report.

- See whether any bank accounts appear that you have not opened.

- See whether the public records section lists any tax liens, bankruptcies, or default judgments against you.

- Check for any misspelled words, wrong birthdays.

EXCERPT FROM PERSONAL CREDIT REPORT

Loan Type: CREDIT CARD

Late Payment* (36 months)	30	60	90
	0	0	0

Last 36 months	OK dec	OK nov	OK oct	OK sep	OK aug	OK jul	OK jun	OK may	OK apr	OK mar	OK feb	OK jan	OK '05
	OK dec	OK nov	OK oct	OK sep	OK aug	OK jul	OK jun	OK may	OK apr	OK mar	OK feb	OK jan	OK '04
	OK dec	OK nov	OK oct	OK sep	OK aug	OK jul	OK jun	OK may	OK apr	OK mar	OK feb	OK jan	OK '03

* Number of payments late thirty, sixty, and ninety days.

Adapted from personal credit report from TransUnion.

CONTACTING THE THREE CREDIT RATING BUREAUS

If you want to learn more about the three credit rating bureaus, or if you need to contact them:

Equifax	www.equifax.com	1-800-525-6285
Experian	www.experian.com	1-888-397-3742
TransUnion	www.transunion.com	1-800-680-7289

On the previous page you will see an actual portion of my credit report for one of my credit cards (with credit card name and account number removed), reporting my payment history for the last thirty-six months:

Other Reasons You Can Obtain a Free Report

In addition to the free annual credit report that each company is required by law to provide, you can request an additional free report during the year if any of the following is true about you:

- Credit has been denied by a company.
- Insurance has been denied.
- Employment has been denied.
- You are unemployed and plan to look for a job within sixty days.
- Your credit report is inaccurate.

PROTECTING YOURSELF WITH INSURANCE

Great, just what we all need . . . another insurance premium to pay each month or year. Now, don't misunderstand what I am saying. I believe that insurance is an important part of any financial plan. I was a victim of Hurricane Katrina. My home and office received significant damage, and I am very thankful for insurance.

At this time, I am not so convinced that identity theft insurance is as necessary as property, health, life, or disability insurance. However, you sure don't get that impression from the companies selling identity theft insurance.

It's ironic that many of the companies that are supposed to be protecting you are the companies selling you insurance to protect you. So in essence they are saying, "We aren't doing what we are supposed to be doing, so we will sell you insurance to protect you."

Money magazine had an interesting article on identity theft insurance. Pat Regnier wrote, "A few of them might be useful for some folks. But before you shell out one thin dime, take a deep breath and try to understand what the real risks are—and what's just lurid hype."[1]

Let me summarize several factors as you weigh identity theft insurance.

Determine Your Level of Risk

The first question you should be asking is, "What is my level of risk?" Fortunately, issuers of credit cards as well as debit and ATM cards will hold you liable for a low amount of unauthorized charges if you notify them quickly (usually sixty days or less). This reduces your level of risk for these three types of losses, which lessens the need for identity theft insurance.

Here is your responsibility for reporting loss on each type of card.

Credit Card Risk

According to the FTC Web site (www.ftc.gov), "The Fair Credit Billing Act establishes procedures for resolving billing errors on your credit card accounts, including fraudulent charges on your accounts. The law also limits your liability for unauthorized credit card charges to *$50 per card*" (emphasis added).

However, you must inform the creditor in writing within sixty days of when the creditor mailed your bill. For specific details, go to www.ftc.gov/bcp/conline/pubs/credit/idtheft.htm.

Debit and ATM Card Risk

Also according to the FTC Web site, when you have a loss or theft of either your debit or ATM bank card and you report the loss or theft, your liability may be limited. Specifically:

- If you report it within two business days or discovery, *your loss is limited to $50.*

- If you report it after two days, but within sixty days, *your loss is limited to $500.*

- If you report it after sixty days, *your loss has no limit.*

Bank Account Risk (online and traditional)

In general terms, the rules for debit and ATM cards also hold true for bank accounts. Check with your local bank to request their policies. In most cases the sixty-day notice is very important. This seems to be when your liability greatly increases with credit card companies, financial institutions, and banks.

Identity Theft Insurance: It's Not Full Protection

Most identity theft insurance is basically a credit card monitoring service. They can report to you that someone has opened a credit card account in your name, but they cannot prevent someone from opening an account in your name. Credit card monitoring services cannot report that someone is taking money out of your bank account, nor can they report someone was arrested and gave the police your name and address.

Even though most identity theft insurance policies are only monitoring services, an increasing number of insurers now offer a reimbursement for financial loss and legal bills. Check with your insurance agent to see whether the company offers identity theft coverage with your homeowner's or renter's insurance policy. You might find that some companies will cover financial losses up to $25,000 for as little as $50 per year. Identity theft insurance typically sells from $50 to $120 a year as a rider to these policies.

Prior to adding this coverage, however, be sure to check out the list of questions below in the section "Before You Buy, Read the Fine Print."

After the Fact

Remember, most credit card monitoring services only inform you after something has happened; they cannot prevent a theft. A company that monitors your credit report and credit cards cannot stop someone from opening up a credit card in your name. It *can* inform you that a new account has been opened. Yes, you can stop the crime from continuing—but you cannot prevent the crime.

If it would help you sleep better at night and you can afford the premium, go ahead and buy it. However, please fully understand what you are buying.

Before You Buy, Read the Fine Print

Before you purchase identity theft insurance, know exactly what you are purchasing. In other words, *read the fine print.* Here are some of the questions that you should be asking before you purchase identity theft insurance:

- How often will my account be monitored for activity? Daily? Weekly? Monthly?
- How will I be informed of account activity?
- Will all three credit bureaus be monitored or just one?
- How often can I access my credit report without being charged a fee?
- How much will the insurance company pay for expenses related to identity theft?
- Exactly what types of expenses will be reimbursed?
- Will loss of income from having to miss work be reimbursed?
- What is the deductible?
- Does the company offer a hotline help service?
- Does the company fill out "all" the forms for me?
- Does the company provide legal service?

My advice is to ask lots of questions, and if you don't see it in print, don't assume you have a specific coverage.

AVOIDING SCAMS

Being aware of the most common financial scams is a very important component in building your wall of protection. Most financial scams are attempts by thieves to make you reveal personal data. Be sure to review the list of the "top ten scams" presented in chapter 1 to be alert for these attempts to steal your identity. The more you know about the most common scams, the more prepared you will be to recognize old or new scams coming your way.

ACTION ALERTS

Another building block in establishing a wall of protection is to take preemptive action. The "action alerts" located throughout the book will help you to do that. Pay special attention to each alert. My action alerts in no way minimize all the other protection ideas presented in the book, of course. Still, you should give immediate priority to the recommendations that I have labeled "action alerts." Indeed, they are more than recommendations, for in most cases they can alert you to a weakness in the wall and help you reinforce that wall of protection.

ON ALERT

The final brick in establishing a wall of protection is to have an alert attitude. You and I need to be "on alert" concerning identity theft and financial scams. Unfortunately, being on alert needs to become a *way of life* for all of us. I say "unfortunately" because continually being on alert typically will increase the level of stress in a person's life.

We live in a rapidly changing financial world. The way we are doing business and making financial transactions has changed in the past ten years. We must adapt to protect ourselves.

For example, we need to *scrutinize* every e-mail,

every phone call, and every conversation that involves our finances or personal data/information. We need to be *cautious* when a person asks for our Social Security number. We need to be *vigilant* in monitoring our bank, investment, and credit card accounts. We need to be *methodical* in requesting free credit reports once every four months.

Because we are living in an unprotected world, we need to learn how to continually protect ourselves. No one should be more concerned about protecting you than . . . you! You are the first line of defense against identity theft, so *continually be on the alert.*

But, even if you are constantly on the alert, there are some things that are 100 percent out of your control.

THINGS OUT OF YOUR CONTROL

We should be doing everything we can to protect our good name, but in the area of identity theft there are some things we can protect and some things that are totally out of our control. Yes, adding the twenty preventives in chapters 4–6 will help you build a wall of protection around your financial life. But some areas are totally out of your control—and might lead to some form of identity theft. Be alert to these.

For example, you have no control over information obtained about you in the following situations:

1. Data stolen from a business by an employee or hacker
2. Data lost or misplaced by a business or data storage company
3. Data breaches that take place in large companies

4. Data being obtained by a crook bribing an employee to obtain information
5. Data being obtained by a hacker breaking into a company computer system

Don't spend your time worrying about things that you cannot control. If someone steals your identity, when you find out, you can deal with it then. In the cases of situations 1–3, companies and business that experience security lapses often will work with their customers, notifying them and often providing free credit monitoring service for the short term (up to three months) to help customers watch for misuse of their credit.

REVIEWING YOUR OWN WALL OF PROTECTION

How does your wall of protection look today? Have you laid the first brick, or is your wall of protection fully built? You must become proactive in protecting yourself

Your Wall of Protection

ID Insurance	Avoiding Scams	Action Alerts	Being on Alert
Your Statements	Credit Cards	Unsolicited Mail	Credit Reports
While Traveling	On Telephone	Your Investments	In Public Places
Writing Checks	ID Cards	Applications	U.S. Mail
At Home	At Work	Your Computer	On the Internet

from identity theft. Learn how to begin protecting your-self as you live in an unprotected world.

The "Action Checklist" at the end of this book pro-vides a summary checklist of all the means of protection we have discussed in this book. This checklist will *not guarantee* your identity will not be stolen, but your level of security will be greatly increased!

In the next chapter I will be outlining exactly what you need to be doing in the unfortunate case someone has stolen your good name.

NOTES

1. Pat Regnier, "Are You Terrified About Identity Theft Yet?" *Money*, September 2005, 114.

SEVEN

The Recovery

HOW DO YOU REPORT ID THEFT
AND RECLAIM YOUR GOOD NAME?

THE IDEAL IS THAT WE PREVENT the theft of our identity, and the previous chapter shows you how. But what happens if you are a victim of identity theft? The goal is recovery of any financial losses, your emotions, and your good name. But as Judy's touching story in chapter 2 proves, that can be difficult. What I learned from talking to victims of identity theft (and reading their stories) is that once they discovered their identity had been stolen, they did not know who to call or what to do. They were frustrated, helpless, confused, and lacked specific direction.

On the following pages you will find a summary of specific steps you need to take if you discover your identity has been stolen. What most victims learned is that they had to take charge of the crisis, because it appeared that no one else really cared or provided help.

Despite that appearance, there really are very helpful Web sites and people who are willing to help. You will find most of the following information at:

www.consumer.gov/idtheft. You may also call 1-877-ID-THEFT for assistance.

If you learn your identity has been stolen:

STEP 1
CALL A FINANCIAL INSTITUTION(S)

Once you find out that one or more of your accounts (bank, credit card, etc.) have been affected, you need to immediately inform the financial institution. They will walk you through the process of closing the account or issuing new account numbers.

When you call, ask if you can use the standard ID Theft Affidavit when filing your written report. (I will tell you where you can obtain the ID Theft Affidavit later in this chapter.)

Inform them that you are in the process of filing a report with the police and the Federal Trade Commission (FTC).

STEP 2
CONTACT A CREDIT BUREAU

Contact one of the big three credit bureaus, Equifax, Experian, or TransUnion. Whether by Internet or a telephone call, you want to accomplish three things: (1) register for a fraud alert, (2) request a security freeze, and (3) request a copy of your credit report.

1. Register for Fraud Alert

All you have to do to register for a fraud alert is contact *one* of the three major credit bureaus; they are required by law to inform the other two bureaus about the alert. You can reach them either online or by phone.

BUREAU	WEB SITE	PHONE
Equifax	www.equifax.com	1-800-525-6285
Experian	www.experian.com	1-888-397-3742
TransUnion	www.transunion.com	1-800-680-7289

A fraud alert lets creditors know it's possible you have been a victim of identity theft. Creditors are to follow specific steps to help protect you and make it difficult for someone to obtain new credit in your name. The three credit bureaus will "flag" your account with a "fraud alert" and a "victim's statement." You do not have to prove that your identity has been stolen, but you must suspect you have been or are about to be a victim. For example, if your wallet or purse has been stolen or you responded to a "phishing" scam e-mail, or your credit card bill did not show up in the mail as scheduled—you are at high risk for identity theft.

According to an FTC survey, only 2 percent of those responding said additional accounts were opened in their name after a fraud alert was placed on their account.[1]

Your fraud alert can be either an initial or extended alert. You can register *an initial alert* if you suspect you have been or potentially will be a victim of identity theft. You can obtain this alert by phone or on the Web site. You can register *an extended alert* if you determine you actually are a victim of identity theft. Do so by completing the identity theft report. The identity theft report should include as much information as you can provide about the crime. For more information about filing the identity theft report, visit www.consumer.gov/idtheft.

Once a fraud alert is placed on your account, no new account supposedly can be opened until the company opening the account or granting credit contacts you directly. I say "supposedly" because not every business does a credit check before granting credit, so they might not even know about your fraud alert. When signing up for the fraud alert, you might want to provide them with your cell phone number so that it will be easier for them to contact you.

ACTION ALERT

OBTAINING A FRAUD ALERT

If you have been a victim of a fraud alert—or even suspect you have been a victim—you should move to quickly alert the three credit bureaus of the situation. In most cases, this will prevent new credit accounts from being opened unless the company contacts you directly and receives your permission. Here are the two types of fraud alerts and how to get them:

TYPE OF ALERT	HOW TO OBTAIN	LENGTH OF ALERT
An Initial Alert. If you suspect you have been or potentially will be a victim of identity theft	Obtain by phone call or Web site	Remains on your file for ninety days
An Extended Alert. If you determine you have been a victim of identity theft	Obtained by filing a written identity theft report	Remains on your file for seven years

2. Request a Security Freeze (if possible)

Some states allow individuals to place a "security freeze" on their credit reports. This is better than a fraud alert, because it prevents anyone from accessing your credit report for any reason. The only exception is if you unfreeze your report. It is practically impossible to obtain a new credit card, obtain a new loan, or sign up for a new cell phone without a credit report. So you can see how this can prevent many forms of fraud.

A security freeze is free to identity theft victims, while nonvictims who desire to freeze their credit report are required to pay a small fee. As of the writing of this book, a security freeze is only available in a few states.

3. Request a Copy of Your Credit Report

Whether you file an initial fraud alert or an extended alert, you are entitled to copies of your credit reports at no charge from the three credit reporting agencies.

STEP 3
FILE A POLICE REPORT

Your local police department may tell you this is unnecessary, but insist on filing a police report. Some states require that police stations file your report. If an officer simply will not file a report, ask to file a "Miscellaneous Incidents" report. You can also check with the attorney general's office in your state to find out what report the police are required to file in your state (if any). To find the office and number for your state's attorney general, go to www.naag.org.

Once the police report has been filed, request a copy of the report for your records.

It is very important to document exactly what happened in your police report. Give as many specific details and facts as possible. Provide any relevant dates, times, companies, and names of people as possible. Explain how you found out about the crime, specifically what you have done and whom you have talked to. Be sure to document each fraudulent charge with dates, dollar amounts, and merchants.

If the police department will not accept your report, type up your own report and document all the details (who, what, when, why, and how). Be sure you keep a copy of all your reports for future use.

STEP 4
FILE IDENTITY THEFT
COMPLAINT WITH THE FTC

Next you need to register your complaint with the FTC. You can file the ID Theft Complaint with the Federal Trade Commission by telephone, Internet, or mail. Call the FTC at 1-877-ID-THEFT; or visit the Web site: www.consumer.gov/idtheft; or mail your complaint to

> Identity Theft Clearinghouse
> Federal Trade Commission
> 600 Pennsylvania Ave. NW
> Washington, DC 20580

Your case will be entered into the FTC's "Consumer Sentinel" database, a nationwide list of ID theft cases. This data will be used to help catch criminals.

Be sure you document in writing everything you report.

STEP 5
COMPLETE AN ID THEFT AFFIDAVIT

You need to send the ID Theft Affidavit to all of the companies, financial institutions, and credit bureaus you contacted in step #1. Most will allow you to print out and use the standard ID Theft Affidavit. If they will not allow you to use the standard ID Theft Affidavit, they will provide you with a form provided by their company.

You can find the standard ID Theft Affidavit online at www.consumer.gov/idtheft. The affidavit has two parts:

- *Part One: The ID Theft Affidavit* is where you provide general information about yourself and the theft.

- *Part Two: The Fraudulent Account Statement* is where you provide specific information about accounts opened in your name. You will need to fill out a separate Fraudulent Account Statement for each company you are dealing with.

Be sure to *use certified mail* to mail the forms. Keep any originals (police reports, etc.) and attach copies to your report.

When you have completed the affidavit, mail *a copy to each company or bank* that granted unauthorized credit or transfer of funds. Provide copies of all documentation requested and any other documentation that you believe is relevant to your case.

In addition to the required forms, you should *request in writing that the company provide you with copies of the account application and transactions* that relate to this account. Once you receive the documents, look for "keys to fraud" such as your signature, incorrect birth dates and addresses.

Any *signs of fraud* you discover should be well documented. For example, circle the signature if the signature on the application is not yours. Provide proof of your signature along with this document.

Documentation of your correspondence is important, so send a certified letter with return receipt to each credit reporting company, bank, or credit card company you talk with. Also, *document your phone calls*; include dates, times, and the names of the people you spoke with on the phone. Of course, be sure to retain copies of all documents and correspondence. The importance of documentation cannot be overemphasized. See the Hot Tip "Presenting Your Case" for more on documenting each contact you make.

STEP 6
BLOCK INFORMATION ON
YOUR CREDIT REPORT

If you discover that any incorrect information on your credit report is a result of identity theft, you have the right to request this information be removed (blocked) on your file. Each of the credit agencies will provide you with a "correction of errors" form you will need to submit.

The Fair Credit Reporting Act requires that any incorrect information be removed (or blocked) on your record, unless the credit issuer can prove the information is indeed correct. You also have the right to correct any incorrect information (birth date, employer, address, phone number, etc.) provided by the thief that is on your record.

HOT TIP

PRESENTING YOUR CASE

Remember as you seek a satisfactory resolution to always (1) know your rights, and (2) be familiar with the FTC recommended steps to resolve a problem.

In all your oral and written communication with a company,

- be assertive (but kind).
- be organized and know the facts when you speak/write to a company.
- be prepared to talk to several people at a company or bank before you will be able to obtain the information you need.

STEP 7
REQUEST LETTER WHEN THE CASE IS SOLVED

If your dispute has been resolved, be sure the company provides you with a letter stating the dispute has been resolved. It is very possible you will need this important document in the future. Do not accept a phone call from the company. Insist that they send you a letter.

STEP 8
MONITOR YOUR PROGRESS

Keep on top of your credit report. You might think all the issues have been resolved, but you need to continually

HOT TIP

DOCUMENTING YOUR CASE

For every bank and credit card account, contact the company and find out what documentation they need submitted.

Carefully document every phone call in a journal. Be sure to include the following:

- the date
- the time
- the person you talked with
- the results—direction given
- a letter that follows up every phone call . The letter should review key points of what was said, as well as reference the date of the call and the results.

Carefully document every written correspondence. To do so, be sure to:

- send all by certified mail with return receipt.
- keep copies of all letters.
- keep copies of all forms you fill out and mail.
- always send copies of supporting documents (keep originals in your file).

Be sure to retain all records (letters, etc.) even after case is resolved. You never know when a related problem might pop up again.

confirm that everything is okay by requesting your free annual report once every four months.

NOTE

1. Federal Trade Commission, "Identity Theft Survey Report," September 2003, 58; www.ftc.gov/os/2003/09/synovatereport. pdf

EIGHT

The Solutions

IS THERE ANYTHING THE GOVERNMENT OR BUSINESSES CAN DO?

EARLIER WE DISCUSSED HOW you can build a wall of protection around your financial life (chapters 4–6). The focus was on "prevention." Prevention is helpful, but everyone is asking, "How can we *solve* identity theft?" Why do we have to spend so much time, energy, money, and effort on prevention, if the problem can be solved on the national level?

Are there really any solutions? Actually, there are many things that business and government could do to help solve identity theft. Only five are listed below.

SOLUTION 1: CREDIT CHECK NOTIFICATION SYSTEM

If I were notified every time someone requested a credit check under my name, I would be able to thwart the plans of the identity thief. Does it not make sense that if someone has the ability to obtain a credit card, buy a car, or obtain a loan in my name, I should have the right to know about it? Think about it. What would be wrong with this system?

When anyone requested a credit check under my name, I should have the option to receive a call or a text message on my cell phone, or an e-mail. If someone has requested a credit check on me, *I have every right to know about it—immediately.* Because if a bank is just about to issue a loan in my name, and I have not applied for a loan, the loan should not be granted. It's really simple. And if the credit bureaus are concerned about the additional administrative cost, just add an additional fee for a credit check. However, in the age of e-mail and text messaging with computers, the cost and administrative burden is minimal.

Currently we have no free notification system in operation; however, some identity theft monitoring insurance programs do offer this service for a fee.

SOLUTION 2: IDENTIFYING WITHOUT SOCIAL SECURITY NUMBERS

The original intent of Social Security numbers was to help administrate the program—not to provide every business in the nation with a national identification system. One option is to require that businesses stop using Social Security numbers for identification.

I have some good news to report in this area. Many businesses have volunteered to create unique identification numbers for their customers. Recently my health insurance company stopped using my Social Security number for identification and issued a new card with a new identification number. The more companies that make this transition, the better!

SOLUTION 3: USE OF BIOMETRICS FOR IDENTIFICATION

Biometrics is the use of personal fingerprints, the iris of the eye, or another unique physical marker to identify individuals. The reason someone can steal your identity is that all they need is your name, address, Social Security number, and a few other pieces of information. What if a business had the means of verifying that the person applying for a loan is actually who they say they are by some distinct biological measurement? For example, no one else in the world has the characteristics of my iris.

SOLUTION 4: ACCOUNT ACTIVITY NOTIFICATION SYSTEM

What if you received a text message on your cell phone every time someone logged in to your bank account or investment account, changed a password, changed your billing address, or requested an additional debit or credit card linked to your account? This would surely help solve the problem.

Identify theft works because the victim becomes aware their identity has been stolen several months after the fact! When we shorten the "awakening" timeline, we eliminate much of the problem.

SOLUTION 5: CREDIT REPORT FREEZE

What if the government provided you the option to put a *freeze* on your credit report? That would mean no one, *including you*, could obtain a credit card, open a bank account, activate a cell phone, or acquire a loan. Of course, most businesses would not grant credit because they could not see your credit report. However, once you have all the credit cards you need, and you don't plan to apply for a mortgage or to buy a car using debt, what does it matter if your account is frozen? It would not only protect against thieves making unwanted credit applications, but it would keep you from applying for an additional, unnecessary credit card.

An ability to freeze your credit report would help to put your personal credit report in a locked file that no one can obtain—including you.

It's hard for me to comprehend why Congress has not passed "credit freeze" legislation to help solve the problem for millions of Americans. Such legislation would still allow you to unfreeze your account later if you determined you needed new credit later. For instance, for seven days you could allow all inquiries; after that, you have the account frozen again. Unfreezing your account would require you to provide your PIN or key fob code, and tell the credit reporting agency how long to unfreeze your account.

THE ARGUMENTS AGAINST SOLUTION 5

This final solution has the potential to make Americans active participants in managing and protecting their credit reports. Yet there is much opposition to it, especially by the credit industry. Here are those arguments and responses to each.

1. Inconvenient

Credit agencies (and their lobbyists) oppose the freeze option because they believe consumers would not like the inconvenience of having to call or log in and temporarily unfreeze their account.

Well, Mr. Lobbyist, why don't you let us make that decision?

2. A Slower Economy

The credit industry also argues that freezes will have a negative impact on the economy and consumer spending. They argue that consumers love the ability to walk into a store, pick out a TV, apply for instant credit, and take it home. A decrease in instant credit translates into fewer sales and a slower economy.

Does that mean that in order to keep the economy strong, all Americans need to remain at identity theft risk? Sounds like it. How stupid is that logic?

3. Consumer Confusion?

Another argument is that the consumer will be confused and frustrated. In other words, the credit industry is saying the average consumer is not smart enough to understand how to freeze and unfreeze his or her account.

You have got to be kidding! This might be an appropriate perspective for many (but not all) senior citizens, but an invalid perspective for the young and middle-age citizens who are becoming more computer and Internet savvy every day.

4. Administrative Burden for Credit Bureaus

Some argue if we allow millions of individuals to freeze and unfreeze their accounts, the administrative expense for the credit bureaus would greatly increase the cost of managing and obtaining credit reports. More staff would be hired, creating increased expenses that would have to be passed on to consumers who have to pay for credit reports.

This one is a very weak argument. In the age of advancing technology (especially automated telephone access, computers, and the Internet), there would be little administrative burden. Thousands, if not millions, of consumers could be logging in daily to freeze or unfreeze their accounts without one human having to do anything. Indeed, thousands of companies—banks, brokerage houses, and other institutions—now allow customers to go online and "manage their accounts" by checking or unchecking a box. Not one person has to be hired to answer the phone or manually change any records.

5. Time-consuming for Consumers

Another argument is that account freezes would become too time-consuming for consumers. Opponents of offering credit freezes say it would just take too long for consumers to freeze and unfreeze their accounts.

Give me a break. How long does it take to log on to a Web site and check a few buttons? Compare the few minutes it might take to freeze or unfreeze an account to the hundreds of hours it takes to resolve an identity theft problem.

Draconian

One lobbyist opposed to this new legislation called freezes the most "dramatic and draconian alteration" to hit the system. *Draconian* means extremely severe or cruel.[1]

What rhetoric! Who is being the cruel one here? This argument, like the previous ones, is a *lame excuse* for derailing the move to an important line of defense against identity theft, a security freeze on your credit reports.

AN OPTION TO CONSIDER

If consumers were surveyed, I am convinced that more than 99 percent would love to have the *option* to freeze their account if it could virtually prevent identity theft! Let me emphasize that this is an option. No one is demanding that everyone use the "account freeze option." It can be 100 percent optional for every consumer.

Come on, credit bureaus. Come on, financial institutions. Come on, lobbyists. Give us the option to freeze our credit report accounts and take a giant step in helping to solve identity theft!

A credit report freeze as well as the other proposed solutions suggest that identity theft related to credit cards, banks, and loans is a solvable problem.

We need a national solution. The time is now for businesses and government to act and help solve the fastest-growing crime in America—identity theft.

NOTE

1. Associated Press, "Credit Bureaus Shun Identity Theft Weapon," August 30, 2004; http://msnbc.msn.com/id/5841962/print/1/displaymode/1098.

Helpful Resources

WHERE CAN I LEARN MORE?

REMEMBER THE OLD YELLOW PAGES slogan, "Let your fingers do the walking . . . through the Yellow Pages"? Well, we live in an information world that goes far beyond important information found in the yellow pages. Today, with a computer, an Internet connection, and a couple clicks of a mouse, we can have information on practically any topic in a matter of seconds.

Here are more than a dozen Web sites, as well as several telephone numbers, to get you started in protecting yourself in this unprotected world. Through key Web addresses you can obtain information, forms, even booklets with the click of a mouse.

On my Web site, www.foundationsforliving.org, you will find all the Web sites listed below and more. All you will have to do is click on the link provided and it will take you directly to the Web site.

www.ftc.gov ....

The above Web site is the home page of the Federal Trade Commission. The FTC has a great Web site. You will be able to find lots of important information on their site, not only about identity theft but other topics. If you are looking for information about identity theft, just click on the link you see on the home page.

What I like about the site:

It's a great government-hosted Web site—and you should be able to trust the information you find on it.

www.consumer.gov/idtheft ....

The above Web site is hosted by the Federal Trade Commission. In fact, the home page reads, "Welcome to the Federal Trade Commission: Your National Resource About Identity Theft."

You can also call them at: 1–877–IDTHEFT

What I like about the site:

This is the Web site you use to file a complaint about identity theft. All you have to do is fill out a simple form to register your case. Your information goes into a national database. I urge you to visit this site if your identity has been stolen—or just to learn more about identity theft.

The site also gives you a specific list of everything you need to do if your identity has been stolen or you want to report suspicious e-mails, phone calls, or letters.

You will also find a thirty-four page identity theft guide on the site. You can read the guide online or print and consult it as needed.

www.annualcreditreport.com ....

This is the Web site you need to use when requesting your free credit report. You are allowed by law to request one credit report annually from the three credit reporting companies. It is recommended that you request one free report every four months, instead of requesting all three at one time.

What I like about the site:

This is the only Web site you have to visit in order to request your free credit report. All three credit reporting companies are linked to this one-stop Web site.

www.idtheftcenter.org ....

This Web site is hosted by the Identity Theft Resource Center, a nonprofit organization located in San Diego. Its stated purpose is "Helping People Prevent and Recover from Identity Theft."

What I like about the site:

The site includes an extensive list of scams with detailed information. It also has a great victim resource center complete with sample letters you can use. The frequently asked questions provide some great information. You will also find a link to a listing of all the current identity theft laws.

www.privacyrights.org ....

The Privacy Rights Clearinghouse, which describes itself as a "nonprofit consumer information and advocacy organization," includes fact sheets, FAQs, and speeches and testimony by PRC officials at this Web site.

What I like about the site:

It's very user-friendly, with a great home page index and links to various topics. You can spend hours on this site learning about identity theft and privacy rights.

800-269-0271 ....

This is the Social Security Administration fraud line. You can also find information on fraud against Social Security recipients at **www.ssa.gov.**

www.usdoj.gov/criminal/fraud/idtheft.html ....

Sponsored by the U.S. Department of Justice, this Web site answers many questions about identity theft.

What I like about the site:

I like the fact that this is hosted by the U.S. Department of Justice. It's a very simple site—not a lot of fluff, bells, and whistles. The site also provides numerous links to other government and private Web sites.

www.fbi.gov/ ....

The FBI Web site represents another helpful government-hosted home page on the topic of identity theft. Type in "identity theft" on the search line and you can access scores of articles from the "Press Room" archives, including articles on identity theft crimes the FBI has solved.

What I like about the site:

Just having the word *FBI* on the top of the page adds credibility to the articles or press releases. You will find press releases, reports, scam alerts, and some very interesting reading.

One very interesting article I recommend is "No Ordinary Case of Identity Theft," found at www.fbi. gov/page2/oct04/uncoveridt101504.htm.

www.ic3.gov ....

The Internet Crime Complaint Center (IC3) is a partnership between the FBI and the National White Collar Crime Center to address fraud committed over the Internet. "IC3's mission is to serve as a vehicle to receive, develop, and refer criminal complaints regarding the rapidly expanding arena of cyber crime. The IC3 gives the victims of cyber crime a convenient and easy-to-use reporting mechanism that alerts authorities of a suspected criminal or civil violation. For law enforcement and regulatory agencies at the federal, state, local, and international level, IC3 provides a central referral mechanism for complaints involving Internet related crimes."

What I like about the site:

It's very impressive. In their press room you will find a list of new and old scams being used. You'll find great statistical information for current and past years. You will find alerts about scams including the infamous Nigerian e-mail, and the fraudulent e-mail posing as a letter from the Red Cross or FBI, and even a scam using the death of the pope to defraud people.

www.aarp.org/bulletin/consumer ....

This is the AARP online consumer alert Web site. A major purpose of this site is to provide a listing of known scams.

What I like about the site:

When I visited the site there were more than forty scam alerts highlighted on the home page, with detailed descriptions available. The AARP site contains very helpful and interesting reading. It is hard to believe the variety of ways dishonest people will take advantage of the poor, the sick, the disabled, and senior citizens. I would hate to be standing in their shoes on judgment day.

www.antiphishing.org ....

The Anti-Phishing Working Group is an industry association composed of financial institutions, online retailers, Internet service providers, and the law-enforcement community. Its stated purpose is "eliminating the identity theft and fraud that result from the growing problem of phishing and email spoofing."

What I like about the site:

This is a great Web site for understanding phishing, explaining current statistics, and reporting phishing incidents.

www.whitepages.com ....

It's a free telephone directory for the nation! If someone gives you his telephone number (or if you have caller ID that displays the number), you can verify the business or person that phone number represents.

What I like about the site:

You can type in the name for just about any person and business, and if they have a listed phone number, you can find it. So if you want to investigate whether the business exists and you have obtained the business name and its state (ask for the state where its headquarters are), you can locate its phone number at whitepages.com. Unlisted telephone numbers will not be shown at this Web site, of course, but most legitimate businesses should have listed numbers; if not, beware. You can also do a reverse search. If you have the phone number, you can type it in and find out who the number belongs to. Again, if it's unlisted, beware.

www.bbb.org ....

The Better Business Bureau is a name we all have learned to respect. Since its beginning in 1912, the Better Business Bureau now has more than one hundred fifty branches throughout the United States, seeking "to promote and foster the highest ethical relationship between businesses and the public through voluntary self-regulation, consumer and business education, and service excellence."

What I like about the site:

The Web site bbb.org is loaded with great information that you can trust. You will not only find helpful information about identity theft, but great information in other areas of interest.

www.ftc.gov/os/2003/09/synovatereport.pdf ......

This Web site provides an online copy of the FTC's 2003 Identity Theft Survey. You can download and print a copy. This FTC-sponsored national survey on identity theft and the experiences of the victims is entitled "Federal Trade Commission—Identity Theft Survey Report."

What I like about the site:

If you like reading, you will find this ninety-three-page government report very informative. It's full of summary facts and figures about identity theft.

http://financialservices.house.gov ....

This is one of the many Web sites reporting on the activities of Congress and its committees. This specific Web site is for the House Committee on Financial Services.

What I like about the site:

By doing a search on "identity theft" you will be able to find past and proposed legislation by Congress. You will also find current press releases and transcripts of congressional hearings.

www.equifax.com ....
www.experian.com ....
www.transunion.com ....

In chapter 6 I introduced you to these three Web sites and gave you telephone numbers to report suspected ID fraud. The three credit reporting agencies are also a great resource to order credit reports—just keep in mind that you are entitled to one *free report* from each agency per year, but only through the Web site www. annualcreditreport.com.

Here is the contact information for these credit bureaus to receive an additional credit report or to contact them by mail:

Equifax	**Experian**	**TransUnion**
800-685-1111	888-397-3742	800-916-8800
P.O. Box 740241	P.O. Box 9532	P.O. Box 6790
Atlanta, GA 30374-0241	Allen, TX 75013-9532	Fullerton, CA 92834-6790

Action Checklist

THOSE WHO KNOW ME WELL know that I love simplicity. In this chapter I am attempting to summarize all of the suggestions, action alerts, and prevention ideas listed in the book. Let me suggest that you use this chapter to personally analyze your level of risk. (The corresponding page number is shown in parentheses following the suggestion.)

The more items you can check off your list, the more likely your wall of protection will keep someone from stealing your identity or committing financial fraud.

❑ 1. Have a good shredder available to use at your home (page 58).

❑ 2. Have a good shredder available to use at your work (page 62).

❑ 3. Shred all your mail (page 58).

❑ 4. Never recycle your financial mail (page 59).

❑ 5. Use caution when around those with financial problems (page 10).

❏ 6. Use a locking file cabinet at your home (page 60).

❏ 7. Use a locking file cabinet at your work (page 62).

❏ 8. Install antivirus software on your computer (page 64).

❏ 9. Install firewall software on your computer (page 64).

❏ 10. Update your antivirus and firewall software daily (page 64).

❏ 11. Regularly download patches for your computer when available (page 65).

❏ 12. Use two computers if financially possible (page 65).

❏ 13. Don't keep your computer "online" twenty-four hours a day (page 65).

❏ 14. Use a wipe-clean software when you dispose of a computer or when you delete files (page 66).

❏ 15. Don't download files from strangers or unsolicited e-mails (page 69).

❏ 16. Don't download free software (page 69).

❏ 17. Create strong passwords used for log-in (page 71).

❏ 18. Don't use the automatic log-in feature when on the Internet (page 72).

❏ 19. Always "log out" of Web sites (page 72).

❏ 20. Use a key chain fob if available (page 73).

❏ 21. Delete temporary Internet files on a regular basis (page 73).

❏ 22. Try to avoid using wireless connection when viewing financial data online (page 74).

❏ 23. Never open e-mail file attachments sent to you by strangers (page 75).

❏ 24. Never click on links in e-mails unless you know the person providing the link and know that it does not relate to financial data (page 75).

❏ 25. Never send personal data such as credit card numbers in a regular e-mail (page 75).

❏ 26. Never send any confidential information that you would not want someone else to read in a regular e-mail (page 75).

❏ 27. Be suspicious of official-looking e-mail from banks or credit card companies (page 76).

❏ 28. Check Web site address to make sure it's the official and not a bogus Web address (page 78).

❏ 29. Know the signs of a secure Web site (icon lock and *https*; page 78).

❏ 30. Do not respond to pop-up ads by clicking on "yes" (page 79).

❏ 31. Do not respond to "warnings" that pop up and ask if you want your computer scanned for viruses (page 79).

❏ 32. Do not click on unsubscribe links unless you know the company is valid (page 81).

❏ 33. Talk with your kids about cautions when using the computer online (page 82).

❏ 34. Do not print your Social Security number on checks (page 84).

❏ 35. Consider using an initial for your first name on printed checks (page 85).

❏ 36. Consider using a P.O. Box for your address on printed checks (page 86).

❏ 37. Don't write your credit card number on the memo line when paying your bill (page 86).

❑ 38. Consider using a debit card and stop writing checks (page 87).

❑ 39. Change your driver's license number if it is the same as your Social Security number (page 88).

❑ 40. Never carry your Social Security card in your wallet (pages 88, 93).

❑ 41. Store your Social Security card in a safe place (pages 88, 94).

❑ 42. Do not print your Social Security number on a résumé (page 90).

❑ 43. Ask why your Social Security number is needed on applications (page 90).

❑ 44. Be sure to mail from a secure site—not an open mailbox at work (page 91).

❑ 45. Consider installing a secure mailbox at your home (page 92).

❑ 46. Consider asking your employer to install locked mailboxes at work (page 92).

❑ 47. When traveling, place a temporary "hold" on your mail (page 93).

❑ 48. Inform trusted neighbors when you are traveling to remove any packages delivered to your home (page 93).

❑ 49. Clean your wallet of unnecessary cards before traveling (page 93).

❑ 50. When traveling consider using a preloaded cash card (page 94).

❑ 51. Do not leave personal data or papers on a desk or bed in hotel rooms (page 94).

❑ 52. Keep your hotel key card when you check out (page 94).

☐ 53. Never provide any personal data to anyone calling you on the phone (page 95).

☐ 54. Never provide any personal data to anyone requesting it in an e-mail (page 77).

☐ 55. When in public, cover the keypad with your hand when you type in PIN or other personal data (page 98).

☐ 56. Remember, the government does not endorse any companies (page 97).

☐ 57. Speak softly when providing personal data in a public place (page 98).

☐ 58. Do not leave your purse in an unsecured location at work (page 63).

☐ 59. Reconcile your bank statement every month (page 100).

☐ 60. Review your credit card statement every month (page 100).

☐ 61. Limit the number of credit cards you own and carry to two (page 102).

☐ 62. Don't sign the back of your credit card; instead write "Photo ID Required" on the signature line (page 102).

☐ 63. Maintain low credit limits on your cards (page 103).

☐ 64. Use one credit card for online purchases (page 103).

☐ 65. Keep credit card bills and receipts in a secure location once bill is paid (page 103).

☐ 66. Call credit card companies to opt out of pre-approved credit card offers (page 104).

☐ 67. Call your credit card company to stop convenient checks being sent to you (page 105).

ACTION CHECKLIST

❏ 68. Order a free annual credit report once every four months, one from each of the three credit reporting agencies (page 107).

❏ 69. Only use www.annualcreditreport.com to order your free credit report—no other site! (page 109).

❏ 70. If you purchase identity theft insurance, be sure you read the fine print (page 117).

❏ 71. Request from your financial institution a brochure outlining your level of risk for various types of financial fraud (page 116).

❏ 72. Stay on the alert—continually (page 120).

❏ 73. If your identity has been stolen, *report* it immediately; follow the steps provided (pages 124–132).

❏ 74. If your identity has been stolen, carefully document every correspondence with each institution (page 132).

❏ 75. If you are in favor of credit report account freeze option—contact your state and federal officials and let them know (page 136).

GLOSSARY OF TERMS

Active technology: A Web site or transmission point that requires interaction of some form for each electronic transaction. For example, you have to swipe your card, punch in your PIN, or type in your card number. (See *passive technology*.)

ACH: Automated Clearinghouse; handles electronic transactions for direct deposit and auto-pay. For more information, go to www.nacha.org.

Alert: To warn of a coming event that has potential for harm or danger; not to alarm.

Annual credit report: Federal law requires that each of the three credit reporting bureaus provide you with one free credit report annually. Monitoring your credit report is a good way to help detect identity theft. Watch out for bogus Web sites and e-mail offering you a free credit report. There is only one Web site to request your free credit report: www.annualcreditreport.com.

Antivirus software: Software that is designed to quarantine, delete, or prevent a destructive computer virus from attacking your computer or network.

ATM: Automatic Teller Machine. Allows you to withdraw cash, check balances, and make transfers. Requires the use of a personal identity number for security.

Automatic log-in: Some Web sites will ask if you want to save your user name and password so that when you visit the sight again you don't have to remember them. It is not recommended to use an automatic log-in feature for obvious security reasons.

Biometrics: The use of fingerprints, iris, or a number of other personal identification means. Other examples: hand geometry; voice; gait; signature recognition; thermal imaging.

Check card: Same as debit card; see *debit card*.

Computer patches: Thieves and virus gurus are always looking for new ways to infiltrate or destroy your personal computer. At the same time, the manufacturer of the computer's operating system (for example, Microsoft) is creating solutions and writing computer codes to solve the problem or "patch the hole(s)." Computer patches can usually be downloaded for free online at the manufacturer's Web site.

Contactless payment: The ability to make a purchase or payment without having to physically touch any device. Contactless payment devices are used for toll roads and some gasoline pumps.

Convenience checks: Preprinted checks that credit card companies send you in the mail. When used, the amount of the check (plus fees) goes onto your credit card account. You can call your credit card company and request they "cease delivery of convenience checks."

Cookie: "The main purpose of cookies is to identify users and possibly prepare customized Web pages for them. When you enter a Web site using cookies, you may be asked to fill out a form providing such information as your name and interests. This information is packaged into a cookie and sent to your Web browser which stores it for later use. The next time you go to the same Web site, your browser will send the cookie to the Web server. The server can use this information to present you with custom Web pages. So, for example, instead of seeing just a generic welcome page you might see a welcome page with your name on it." Source: www.webopedia.com

Cracker: (See also *hacker*) One who cracks secure systems, generally with criminal intent—in contrast to a hacker, who generally tries to enter a system to obtain data or to play a prank. Both acts of unauthorized intrusion are crimes.

Credit card: When you make a purchase and use a credit card, the amount of your purchase goes onto your credit card balance. At the end of the month, you are mailed a credit card statement documenting all of your charges. You have the option to pay the bill in full or partially pay what you owe. You can use a credit card and make purchases even if you don't have the money in your bank account to pay for your purchase. (Also see *debit card*.)

Credit card fraud: This fraud occurs when a person obtains your credit card number and uses it to make a fraudulent purchase. Just because someone steals your credit card number and makes a fraudulent purchase *does not mean* that your identity has been stolen. (See *identity theft*.) Congress in the Identity Theft and Assumption Deterrence Act of 1998 instructed the Federal Trace Commission to label credit card fraud as identity theft.

Credit card security code: The four numbers printed on the front (or three numbers on the back) of your credit card are part of a new security code being used by credit card companies. When placing an order on the phone or Internet, not only do you need the credit card number, but you also need the four-digit security code.

Credit report: A report that provides businesses, banks, and credit card companies a summary of your credit history. The report will list your credit cards, balance on each card, and available credit. It will also disclose your loans, employer, address, and payment history. Federal law allows you to request one free credit report from each of the three credit reporting bureaus once each year.

Credit report freeze: When your credit report is frozen, that means that no one, *including* you, can obtain a copy of your credit report. The ability to "freeze your credit report" would help to put your personal credit report in a locked file that no one can obtain, including you. Then, if you want to unfreeze your account, you would have to call the credit bureau, provide your PIN or key fob chain code, and tell them to unfreeze your account for a set period of time to allow all inquiries. This is only available in a few states at this time.

Debit card: A debit card is sometimes known as a check card. A debit card is linked directly to your checking account. When you make a purchase and use a debit card, the money is immediately (or later in the day) transferred out of your checking account. At the end of each month, your debit purchases will be documented on your bank statement, just like your checks are. (For comparison, see *credit card*.)

Download: Normally used in the context of "downloading a file." Means to open a file attached to an e-mail or a Web site and transfer the data into your computer.

Download patches: See *computer patches*.

Dumpster diving: Looking through another person's trash in order to find personal data such as bank account numbers, old credit card bills, Social Security numbers, birth dates, and investment statements that have been trashed.

E-Commerce: The buying and selling of merchandise on the Internet or with some type of electronic transaction not involving the use of cash.

ETA: Electronic Transfer Account

EFTA: The Electronic Funds Transfer Act (EFTA) is a federal consumer protection law covering electronic transactions. It covers electronic fund transfer products such as bank accounts, debit cards, ATMs, and Internet banking.

EFT: Electronic Funds Transfer

Firewall: A software program designed to prevent unauthorized access to your personal computer or a computer network. Designed to help prevent hackers or crackers from accessing your computer system.

Fraud alert: A fraud alert lets creditors know it's possible you have been a victim of identity theft. Creditors are to follow specific steps to help protect you and make it difficult for someone to obtain new credit in your name. The three credit bureaus will "flag" your account with a "fraud alert" and a "victim's statement." Once a fraud alert is placed on your account, before any new account can be opened, the company opening the account or granting credit is supposed to contact you directly.

Global hot spot: Not available today. In the future you will have the ability to connect to the internet or perform financial transactions from literally any location in the world. (See *hot spot*.)

Hacker/Hacking: (See *cracker*) Someone who achieves unauthorized access to a computer or system.

Hot spot: Usually a heavily populated location (airport, library, college campus, hotel) that allows a wireless Internet connection. It is unlikely, but possible for a thief to intersect your wireless Internet connection and view your personal data.

Identity theft: When a person obtains your name, date of birth, address, and/or Social Security number and uses that data to do one or more of the following: open up credit card account(s) or bank account(s), obtain a fraudulent loan(s), secure a job, or lease rental property. Identity theft is not limited to the list provided above; in the Identity Theft and Assumption Deterrence Act of 1998, Congress labeled credit card fraud as identity theft.

Identity Theft Affidavit: The affidavit has two parts. In part one the victim provides general information about himself and the theft. In part two the victim provides specific information about accounts opened in his or her name. You will need to fill out a separate Fraudulent Account Statement (part two) for each company you are dealing with. Available at www.consumer. gov/idtheft.

Identity theft insurance: Insurance that helps you recover from identity theft. Some policies monitor activity on your credit report, such as any new accounts being opened in your name.

Internet banking: Use of the Internet to make purchases, order checks, pay bills, or transfer funds.

Internet connection: There are three basic ways to connect to the Internet: (1) dial up (phone line); (2) broadband DSL (cable or phone); and (3) wireless (radio frequency).

Key fob: A key fob is a security device that displays a new security code every sixty seconds. If you are trying to log on to a financial Web site that uses a key fob, you would be required to type in your user name, password, and the key fob security code.

Log out: Like shutting the back door when you leave a secure Web site. All secure Web sites have a button or link for you to click on to disconnect.

Pharming: Pronounced "farming." Pharming is when crooks create a bogus Web site and attempt to have you log on to it thinking it is authentic. Their goal is to obtain your personal data such as your Social Security number and credit card number.

Phishing: Pronounced "fishing." A scam in which e-mail is sent requesting the recipient to click on a Web site link and provide private information such as a Social Security number. The e-mail appears to be from a reputable company or financial institution, asking the recipient to update his or her file. (See chapter 4 for techniques of phishing and how to respond to this threat.)

PIN: A personal identity number; you create a unique personal identity number to make any electronic transaction more secure.

Prepaid cards: Money can be stored on a card and used in restaurants or to make purchases. The most common prepay card is a gift card.

Secure Web site: Uses SSL (or Secure Socket Layer) and encrypting data to transfer data over the Internet in a coded or secret message. Most secure Web sites will have the following in their address: *https*. Note the *s* following the *http* and a lock icon in the bottom right-hand corner of the computer screen.

Shoulder-surfing: When someone stands close by and tries to hear or read a person's credit card number and security code by peering over their shoulder. Or the surfer tries to see the person type his or her user name and password into the computer.

Shredder: A machine used to cut a document into small pieces of paper to make it almost impossible for the original document to be reconstructed.

Skimming: Your card is "skimmed" when a thief captures your account number and PIN without stealing your card. The numbers are captured when you run your card through a card reader that a trickster has attached over the actual card reader at an ATM machine, for example.

Smart cards: Card has imbedded a small computer chip that can store names, financial data, passwords, and even e-cash.

Social engineering: When an individual intentionally misleads someone, such as a customer service representative or an administrative assistant, to provide personal information about a customer or account.

Spam: Unsolicited electronic junk mail. Usually sent to thousands of e-mail addresses at one time.

Spyware: Software that secretly gathers user information without the user's knowledge. Spyware is typically loaded onto your computer as a hidden component in free software programs downloaded from the Internet. Once installed on your computer system, the software begins to monitor your activity and sends that information to someone while you are on the Internet. Information about your e-mail addresses, credit cards, passwords, and personal data can be obtained and transmitted.

Strong passwords: Passwords that use a combination of letters and numbers. Weak passwords would be like your mother's maiden name, your birthday, year of birth, or pet's name.

Unsecured mailbox: Mailbox that is not secured by a lock or combination lock. Examples are open mailboxes in offices or a mailbox on your home or next to the street.

URL: Uniform Resource Locator—the Web address that routes you to a specific Web site. For example, the URL for Foundations for Living is www.foundationsforliving.org.

U-Scan: Device that allows you to check yourself out in stores.

Virus: Usually loaded onto your computer when you receive an e-mail (with a virus). A computer virus can reproduce, slow a computer down, destroy the contents of your hard drive, cause your computer to do strange things like turn off, and spread the virus to other computers.

Wipe clean software: Removes all selected files or deleted files from your computer, without the possibility of them ever being restored. In some cases even deleted files can be restored on computers with software designed to restore files.

ABOUT THE AUTHOR

Ethan Pope is president of Foundations For Living, a ministry dedicated to helping people simplify and clarify life issues from a biblical and practical perspective. He is a graduate of Dallas Theological Seminary and a CERTIFIED FINANCIAL PLANNER™, though he has never had a financial planning practice. Ethan is a respected author, speaker, and regular guest on national radio programs. Ethan and his wife, Janet, live in Dallas, TX, and have two adult children.

OTHER BOOKS BY ETHAN POPE:

- *Cashing It In—Getting Ready for a World Without Money* (Moody Publishers)
- *Social Security?—What's In It for You* (Moody Publishers)
- *Creating Your Personal MONEY MAP* (Tyndale House Publishers)
- *There's No Place Like Home* (Broadman & Holman Publishers)
- *How to Be a Smart Money Manager* (Thomas Nelson Publishers)

More Information
Available on the Internet!

Sign Up for
Ethan Pope's

FINANCIAL ALERT ENEWS

at

www.foundationsforliving.org

ADDTIONAL INFORMATION ON:

* *Contacting* Ethan Pope
* *Ordering* resources online
* *Receiving* Foundations For Living publications
* *Inviting* Ethan Pope to speak in your city or church

is also available at
www.foundationsforliving.org

Do you know what Scripture says about the coming cashless society or how it will impact you and your family?

Author Ethan Pope says, "We are on the eve of one of the most significant economic developments in the history of the world." Governments, retailers, and financial institutions have already made major changes worldwide. But the modern technologies used could pose serious threats to our security and privacy.

Ethan Pope teaches you:
—Ways to avoid identity theft
—How a cashless society relates to end times prophecy
—Specific steps on how you and your family can get ready

His evidence and analysis are very convincing! This book demands we stop and take note of what he is saying.
　　　　　　　　　　—Josh McDowell, Founder, Josh McDowell Ministry

Ethan knows God's Word and what it says about money and knows how to share it in an understandable way.
　　　　　　　　　　—Howard Dayton, Co-founder, Crown Financial Ministries

A practical, insightful resource that answers a lot of the questions we've all been asking (and a few more that we haven't thought about).
　　　　　　　　　　—Crawford Loritts, Author, Speaker, Radio Host

Cashing It In
ISBN: 0-8024-0971-7

Financial Alert Series

**Now is the time to prepare
for a retirement
without Social Security.**

Over 90 percent of senior Americans depend on Social Security to some degree. For many of these beneficiaries (two-thirds), it represents more than 50 percent of their income. Yet the system is in serious trouble. "Our Social Security system is headed for a crisis," writes financial expert Ethan Pope. "Social Security is one of the most misunderstood programs in our nation's history. If changes are not made, decreases in benefits are inevitable."

Using simple logic in a well-organized format, Ethan Pope carefully documents:

- The problems threatening Social Security and the half-truths surrounding it
- Where the infamous Trust Fund monies have gone
- The top ten potential solutions, including partial privatization
- Changes in the real meaning of retirement
- A personal financial plan to help you prepare for retirement regardless of what happens to Social Security

Armed with these insights and action steps, you'll be equipped to speak up on this critical issue—and to begin providing for your own retirement needs while there's still time. A must-read book for all ages and income levels.

Social Security?
ISBN: 0-8024-0973-3